WHAT WRONGDOERS DESERVE

**Recent Titles in
Contributions in Psychology**

Human Consciousness and Its Evolution: A Multidimensional View
Richard W. Coan

From AI to Zeitgeist: A Philosophical Guide for the Skeptical Psychologist
N. H. Pronko

Inevitability: Determinism, Fatalism, and Destiny
Leonard W. Doob

The Psychology of Writing: The Affective Experience
Alice Glarden Brand

Medieval Psychology
Simon Kemp

Hesitation: Impulsivity and Reflection
Leonard W. Doob

Culture and the Restructuring of Community Mental Health
William A. Vega and John W. Murphy

The Externalization of Consciousness and the Psychopathology of Everyday
Life
Stephen T. DeBerry

Self-Representation: Life Narrative Studies in Identity and Ideology
Gary S. Gregg

Hostage: Terror and Triumph
James F. Campbell

From the Other Side of the Couch: Candid Conversations with Psychiatrists
and Psychologists
Chris E. Stout

Counseling in the Asia-Pacific Region
Abdul Halim Othman and Amir Awang, editors

WHAT WRONGDOERS DESERVE

THE MORAL REASONING BEHIND RESPONSES TO MISCONDUCT

R. MURRAY THOMAS
AND
ANN DIVER-STAMNES

Contributions in Psychology, Number 21
Paul Pedersen, Series Adviser

GREENWOOD PRESS
Westport, Connecticut • London

Library of Congress Cataloging-in-Publication Data

Thomas, R. Murray (Robert Murray).
    What wrongdoers deserve : the moral reasoning behind responses to
misconduct / R. Murray Thomas and Ann Diver-Stamnes.
        p.   cm.—(Contributions in psychology, ISSN 0736-2714 ; no.
21)
    Includes bibliographical references and index.
    ISBN 0-313-28630-2 (alk. paper)
    1. Justice (Philosophy)—Public opinion.   2. Judgment (Ethics)—
Public opinion.   3. Punishment—Public opinion.   I. Diver-Stamnes,
Ann.   II. Title.   III. Series.
BJ1408.5.T48   1993
172'.2—dc20   93-9322

British Library Cataloguing in Publication Data is available.

Library of Congress Catalog Card Number: 93-9322
ISBN: 0-313-28630-2
ISSN: 0736-2714

First published in 1993

Greenwood Press, 88 Post Road West, Westport, CT 06881
An imprint of Greenwood Publishing Group, Inc.

Printed in the United States of America

∞™

The paper used in this book complies with the
Permanent Paper Standard issued by the National
Information Standards Organization (Z39.48-1984).

10 9 8 7 6 5 4 3 2 1

To
Kaitlin Elizabeth Cortenbach

Contents

Preface

At the outset, readers may find it helpful if we explain what this book is and what it is not.

What It Is. The purpose of our investigation has been to reveal aspects of moral reasoning that underlie the consequences people believe wrongdoers should experience. Our approach has consisted of presenting six cases of wrongdoing to a large number of teenagers and young adults and asking them (1) what consequences they would recommend and (2) why they believe their proposals are appropriate. Then we used the participants' answers as the raw material for constructing a taxonomy to use in categorizing features of people's moral reasoning. Subsequently, we applied the resulting taxonomy in comparing group and individual modes of moral decision making.

What It Is Not. This book is not a survey of the scholarly and professional literature in such fields as moral development, crime and punishment, social custom, or the like. Rather, in our attempt to adopt a fresh approach to our task, we set aside the writings of others and concentrated entirely on the opinions expressed by the respondents in this study. Hence, we derived the taxonomy solely by following our data —by trying to understand the thought processes implied in the participants' judgments of the six cases. As a consequence, the book contains very few references to the work of others. Whenever a reference does appear, it has been chosen simply to illustrate a point we wished to make.

We wish to express our appreciation to a variety of people who contributed significantly to the success of the project. We are particularly indebted to eight educators who collected students' opinions about appropriate consequences for wrongdoers —Patricia Meu Ling Leong, George Petersen, Mohammed Rasheed, Abdul Rasheed, Matt Scanlon, Stephen Stamnes, Randy Sweeney, and Darius K. Jonathan. We also wish to thank the 542 respondents who completed quewtionnaires and the 20 individuals who offered their opinions during interviews, with special thanks to Jonathan Lau, Jeff Sterkel, Kelly Sterkel, and Courtney Thomas.

Part I

The Nature of the Study

One of the most frequent ways people display their moral values is in the consequences they propose for those who violate social rules, laws, or customs. In court cases, assigning consequences is a task for judges and juries. In school, it's a job for teachers, principals, deans, and sometimes fellow students. At home, it's the responsibility of parents, guardians, and older siblings. In the factory or office, it's the duty of a boss—the foreman, the supervisor, or the manager. In the military, it's the task of those who outrank the offender. In sports, it can be the coach, the referee, or perhaps the wrongdoer's teammates. Even people not directly involved in applying consequences commonly express opinions about what should be done to those wrongdoers they see on television, read about in the newspaper, or hear about from their acquaintances.

This book describes a study of such matters through analyzing consequences that people believe wrongdoing deserves.

Our method of investigation advanced through four major stages. The first consisted of presenting a printed opinionnaire to 542 people who were asked to write down the consequences they would suggest for wrongdoers in six cases of people who had violated moral codes. Second, we analyzed the 542 responses in order to create a taxonomy that would usefully accommodate the kinds of answers the opinionnaires contained. Third, based on the resulting taxonomic structure, we interviewed 20 additional respondents in order to learn in greater detail the patterns of overt reasoning people display in assigning consequences for wrongdoing. Finally, we interpreted the results of both the opinionnaires and the interviews to answer the following questions:

1. In such moral incidents as those depicted in our six cases, what diverse rationales or types of moral reasoning may people adduce to support the consequences they would suggest for the wrongdoers in the incidents?
2. How can such rationales or kinds of reasoning be organized into categories that are convenient for comparing different people's conceptions of moral issues? In other words, what sort of taxonomy can be devised to structure rationales that undergird proposed consequences?

3. What are the likenesses and differences among the consequences and rationales
   proposed by respondents from the following social settings in the western
   United State—(a) a metropolitan public high school located in a high-
   crime-rate area, (b) a high school sponsored by a religious order in a small
   city, (c) a teacher-education program in a state university, (d) a high school in
   a small Hawaiian oceanside community, and (e) a metropolitan community
   college in Hawaii? In addition, how do the consequences recommended by
   these American groups compare with those suggested by high-school and
   college students in Saudi Arabia?
4. What are probable sources of the likenesses and differences observed among
   the social groups listed under item 3?
5. What do the opinions expressed by the participants in this study suggest
   about the validity of Gilligan's (Gilligan, 1982; Gilligan, Ward, & Taylor,
   1988) contention that men base their moral judgments on a concept of evenhanded justice, whereas women found their moral judgments on
   considerations of compassionate caring?
6. What can be learned about individual styles of overt moral reasoning as
   revealed in interviews with respondents?
7. What implications might the results of this study hold for moral-education
   programs and for court proceedings?
8. What types of additional research might promote further understanding of
   people's moral-reasoning patterns in their proposals of just deserts?

The book is organized into four parts. Part I, consisting of two chapters, sets
the background of the study—its aims, the construction of the opinionnaire used
for gathering people's ideas about consequences, and significant characteristics of
the groups that participated in the study. Part II, composed of three chapters,
describes the taxonomy created from the responses of participants in this study
and from a limited number of accounts of wrongdoing reported in the daily news.
Part III, containing five chapters, compares group and individual responses to the
six cases of wrongdoing. Part IV offers an overview of the main results of the
study and describes practical applications of the taxonomy as well as further
research possibilities.

1

The Six Cases of Wrongdoing

The significant features of the six moral incidents and the reasons the incidents were constructed in such a fashion can perhaps best be explained if we first describe the six anecdotes, then analyze their contents and identify some of their shortcomings.

THE OPINIONNAIRE

The opinionnaire that respondents filled out was cast in the following form. As the personal-identification items at the top of the form indicate, this version was used with high school students. Suitable changes were made in the identification items when the form was used with groups other than high school students.

Your Opinion of What to Do

We are collecting students' opinions about what they think should be done in six cases of people who either had an accident or broke the law. But first, please give the following information about your age, sex, and year in school.

Write your age: _____ years   Circle your sex: boy   girl

Circle your year in high school: Freshman   Sophomore   Junior   Senior

---

Directions: For each incident below, first read the incident. Second, mark an *X* on the line in front of the action you think is best for that case. Third, explain why you think your solution for the case is a good one.

Incident 1: During World War II, a German army colonel who commanded troops in the country of Yugoslavia in 1943 ordered the killing of 109 Yugoslav partisans that the Germans had captured. At the close of the war, the colonel disappeared. But he was discovered in 1982 in South America, where he had been living under a different name for 37 years. While living in South America he had been known to be a good citizen, never involved in breaking the law. He was then caught by Yugoslav secret agents, who took him back to Yugoslavia to stand trial for his wartime activities. When he arrived for his trial, he was age 73 and sick with a serious kidney disease. He was tried in court and found guilty of having ordered the killings.

Your task is to choose from the following actions the one you prefer in this case and to explain why you prefer that choice.

_____ 1. He should be put to death, as the law provided for such crimes.

_____ 2. He should not be put to death but should be imprisoned for the rest of his life.

_____ 3. He should be allowed to return to his home in South America.

_____ 4. Other (explain)

Tell why you think your choice is the best:

Incident 2: A World War II German army major, who supervised the killing of the 109 Yugoslav partisans, had disappeared after the war. Like the colonel, he was discovered in 1982 in South America when he was age 68. While living in South America, he had enjoyed good health and had become a very rich man by smuggling cocaine and marijuana to North America and to Europe. He was captured by Yugoslav agents and taken to Yugoslavia, where he was tried in court and convicted of supervising the killing of the 109 partisans.

Your task is to choose from the following actions the one you prefer in this case and to explain why you prefer that choice.

_____ 1. He should be put to death, as the law provided for such crimes.

_____ 2. He should not be put to death but should be imprisoned for the rest of his life.

_____ 3. He should be allowed to return to his home in South America.

_____ 4. Other (explain)

Tell why you think your choice is the best:

Incident 3: A 14-year-old girl was selling marijuana to a schoolmate in a hallway at school when she was caught by a teacher. As the teacher grabbed the girl by the arm, the girl stabbed him in the stomach with a knife she carried. The girl was later arrested by the police as a result of a description given by the teacher while he was recovering in the hospital. When the police investigated the girl's background, they reported that she had no father but lived on welfare with her mother and three younger sisters in a one-room apartment.

Your task is to choose from the following actions the one you prefer in this case and to explain why you prefer that choice.

_____1. She should be put in a detention facility for juveniles for at least one year, as is provided in this state for juveniles who sell drugs and who attack people with a weapon.

_____2. She should be allowed to return to her home and school, but only if she reports each week to a probation officer who has been appointed by the court.

_____3. Other (explain)

Tell why you think your choice is the best:

_____

Incident 4: A 13-year-old boy was caught one night by police officers as he stole an auto radio from a car in a parking lot. When the officers started questioning him, the boy hit one officer across the face with the iron pipe he had used to break open the car window, and the blow broke the officer's nose and jaw. After the boy was taken to detention hall for juveniles, a social worker reported that the boy did not live at home but, instead, had left home and now lived in the streets. When the social worker spoke with the boy's parents, they said they had put their son out of the house because they could not control him.

Your task is to choose from the following actions the one you prefer in this case and to explain why you prefer that choice.

_____ 1. The boy should be kept for at least a year in a juvenile detention facility, as provided by law.

_____ 2. The boy should be put in a foster home, be enrolled in school, and report weekly to a probation officer.

_____ 3. Other (explain)

Tell why you think your choice is the best:

_____

Incident 5: A man was angry about his wife divorcing him, so he stopped in a bar on the way home from work. After he had several drinks of whiskey, he started driving home. He ran through a stop sign and crashed into a passing car, seriously injuring both of the women in that car. He himself suffered a broken leg and bruises.

Your task is to choose from the following actions the one you prefer in this case and to explain why you prefer that choice.

_____ 1. The man should be put in jail for at least a year.

_____ 2. The man should not be put in jail, but he should have to pay a $1,000 fine and have to pay the medical costs for the women who were injured in the crash.

_____ 3. The driver should not be put in jail, but he should have his driver's license taken away for a year.

_____ 4. The driver should not be held responsible for the accident and therefore should go free.

_____ 5. Other (explain)

Tell why you think your choice is the best:

_____

Incident 6: A woman who was given medicine for an allergy was warned by her doctor not to drive a car while taking the medicine, because it could make her drowsy and could slow down her movements. But she wanted to go shopping for groceries. When she was driving her car to the market, she failed to slow down at a crossroad and she hit a 12-year-old boy who was riding a bicycle. The boy was badly injured, but the woman was not hurt.

Your task is to choose from the following actions the one you prefer in this case and to explain why you prefer that choice.

_____ 1. The woman should be put in jail for at least a year.

_____ 2. The woman should not be put in jail, but she should have to pay a $1,000 fine and have to pay the medical costs for the boy who was injured in the crash.

_____ 3. The woman should not be put in jail, but she should have her driver's license taken away for a year.

_____ 4. The woman should not be held responsible for the accident and therefore should go free.

_____ 5. Other (explain)

Tell why you think your choice is the best:

_____

THE CASE PATTERNS

An inspection of the patterning of the six cases shows that the first pair represented the most violent crime (killing hundreds of people), the second pair represented the next most violent (stabbing and clubbing), and the third pair —although very damaging (auto crashes)—were not intentionally violent.

Furthermore, whereas the perpetrators of the crimes in the first pair were both males, in the second and third pairs there was a male lawbreaker in one case and a female in the other.

THE CHOICE OF MORAL INCIDENTS

The principal criteria guiding the selection of the six incidents were those of (a) comprehensibility, (b) interest, (c) time feasibility, and (d) relevance for the aims of the study.

The term *comprehensibility* refers to how readily respondents understand the issues posed in the moral incidents. This means that the participants should be acquainted with the vocabulary used and can imagine the incidents occurring in their own society or in societies they have learned about in their study of history or current events. Whereas understanding the first two incidents depended on a passing knowledge of events during World War II, the remaining four were ones that drew on events rather common in the daily lives of respondents in the United States.

The *interest* criterion holds that every moral anecdote should capture the attention of the respondents in a way that motivates them to study each incident with care and to answer all the questions diligently. We assumed that keeping the anecdotes brief, focusing them on readily understood conflicts in people's lives, and requiring the reader to offer an opinion about suitable consequences would fulfill the interest requirement.

The *time-feasibility* standard suggests that the task posed on the opinionnaire could be completed during a single session of 30 to 45 minutes (the amount of time available in a typical school), even by respondents who work rather slowly and ponder each moral issue at length. An initial tryout of moral incidents with high school students indicated that this standard would be met if the number of incidents was limited to six.

The *relevance* criterion is the most complex and thus calls for an extended explanation. We may recall from the introduction to Part I that one aim of the study was to elicit from respondents a diversity of proposed consequences and of rationales in support of those proposals. Two features built into the six incidents were intended to encourage such diversity. First, the six incidents should not all focus on the same moral value. Second, various conditions that might affect people's moral judgments should be included in the anecdotes. Since the distinction between *values* and *conditions* is a crucial factor in the analysis of respondents' answers, it requires the following clarification.

At the core of each value is a moral principle in the form of an unembellished statement of what is right or, in its reciprocal form, what is wrong. Table 1-1 illustrates five such principles that are common to many cultures (Gert, 1970; *Holy Bible*, 1611, Exodus, chap. 20; Thomas, 1989). Principles (*a*) and (*b*) are implied in the first two of our six cases, the pair involving the killing of Yugoslav partisans by members of the German army. In both cases, the principle *respect for human life* (and particularly *do not kill*) is in conflict with *obedience to authority*, a conflict expected to produce a moral dilemma for the German officers involved in the incident. Principles (*a*), (*d*), and (*c*) are at stake

Table 1-1

Representative Moral Principles

Virtues to Be Encouraged	*Transgressions to Be Avoided*
(*a*) *Respect for Human Life*: Everyone should protect others from harm and seek to enhance others' physical and mental well-being.	*Disregard for Human Life*: No one should exploit or harm others, either physically or psychologically.
(*b*) *Obedience to Authority*: Everyone should obey properly constituted officials.	*Disobedience to Authority*: It is wrong to disobey legitimately established officials.
(*c*) *Nurturance*: Everyone should act toward others in ways that protect them and enhance their welfare.	*Exploitation*: No one should treat others in ways that diminish their self-control or their mental and physical health.
(*d*) *Respect for Property*: Everyone should protect others' right to hold and use property to which they have proper legal claim.	*Stealing & Vandalism*: No one should take or use others' property without their permission. Damaging others' property is wrong.
(*e*) *Responsibility*: Everyone should carry out those obligations that he or she incurs through a sense of duty or through recognized law or custom.	*Irresponsibility*: No one should neglect to fulfill obligations that are rightfully incurred by contract or through law or custom.

in the cases of the two teenagers—the girl who stabbed a teacher when she was apprehended selling illicit drugs and the boy who struck the police officer when he was caught stealing a car radio. Principles (*a*) and (*e*) (*do not harm others* and *take responsibility for your own behavior*) are of central concern in the final pair of cases—the man and woman who drove their cars while under the influence of drugs. In summary, then, the six incidents focused on several moral values, with those particular values potentially stimulating respondents in our study to propose diverse consequences for violations of the principles.

Now we proceed with the matter of conditions. In any moral-decision situation, the application of a moral principle is affected by a series of conditions. The presumption here is that rarely, if ever, is any moral principle exercised unconditionally in every life situation to which that principle is relevant. In other words, the way a principle is applied in moral decisions depends on selected circumstances of the particular case at hand. Consider, then, the conditions inserted into the six anecdotes. It is apparent that the cases have been arranged in pairs, with each member of a pair being similar to the other member in some ways and different in others. For instance, cases 1 and 2 were alike in that they involved the same principles (*respect for human life* and *obedience to authority*) and shared three conditions—both cases concerned an identical moral incident from the distant past, and both of the central characters were elderly and were male. However, two conditions on which the cases differed were the present health of the central characters and their behavior since World War II.

Cases 3 and 4 were alike in that each involved a young adolescent committing two illegal acts, the first premeditated (selling illicit drugs, stealing a car stereo) and the second spontaneous (using a weapon to injure a person in authority). However, the cases differed in one of the principles violated (peddling drugs, stealing property) and in two conditions—in the gender of the central characters and in the specific nature of the two teenagers' home lives.

Cases 5 and 6 were similar in regard to the principles of *not injuring others* and *exhibiting caution and responsibility* in relation to drug use. As for conditions, in neither case was the wrongdoing (the auto accident) premeditated. And in both cases the drivers apparently knew ahead of time that the substances they had ingested could alter their judgment and self-control, thereby increasing the probability that they might make a mistake. However, the cases differed from each other in two conditions—the gender of the main actors and the motivation for their ingesting the drugs.

A sampling of frequently applied conditions is offered in Table 1-2.

We paired the anecdotes in such a fashion so as to provide a basis for our speculating about how such principles, and the conditions embedded in them, might affect people's opinions about what consequences were warranted for the kinds of wrongdoing depicted in the cases. How this patterning of principles and conditions influenced our interpretations of people's moral judgments is described at various junctures in Parts II and III.

Table 1-2

Conditions That Often Influence Moral Judgments

Age—young children as compared to adolescents, to young adults, to the middle-aged, and to the elderly

Gender—female as compared to male

State of Health—either physical or mental

Moral Character—the incident of wrongdoing is, or is not, indicative of the wrongdoer's typical moral character and behavior

Time of the Wrongdoing —recent as compared to the distant past

Degree of Damage—the act caused little harm as compared to much harm

Knowledge of Right and Wrong—the degree of the individual's awareness of the propriety and consequences of such behavior

Premeditation—whether wrongdoing was planned ahead of time or was committed on the spur of the moment out of a surge of emotion

Life Circumstances—aspects of the wrongdoer's life that could motivate the individual to engage in misbehavior

Lapse of Time—amount of time passed since the offense was committed

Emotional Stability—offender's emotional state at the time of the misdeed

---

LIMITATIONS OF THE ANECDOTES

As stimuli to evoke people's suggestions about consequences for wrongdoing, the six opinionnaire cases exhibit at least three significant shortcomings.

Perhaps the most obvious is the narrow range of moral principles and conditions they encompass. Among dozens of moral values and hundreds of contingencies that can influence people's application of their values, only a handful are addressed in our half-dozen anecdotes. We did not imagine that these six would reveal the entire complexity of ways people assign consequences, but we did expect that the six would provide a sufficient range of raw material on which to ground the sort of taxonomy of consequence assignments that we wished to produce. We assume that future studies can utilize moral incidents focusing on other principles and other consequences so as to further elaborate our initial version of the taxonomy.

A second limitation is that the anecdotes confront respondents only with hypothetical dilemmas. The values people express in such fictitious circumstances may not be identical to those that guide respondents' judgments when they actually are responsible for meting out consequences in daily life, as is required of jury members in court, of parents at home, and of teachers in the classroom. Therefore, it is important to interpret people's responses to the six anecdotes as "expressed opinions about hypothetical cases" and not necessarily "the actual value judgments on which their real-life behavior would be founded." Since the conditions of real life always differ to some extent from those in fiction, it is difficult to quantify the degree to which such expressed values influence individuals' real-life actions. Despite this caveat, we are assuming that there is some connection between the values reflected in answers to hypothetical cases and the values that guide people's daily behavior.

Finally, presenting the cases in the form of a questionnaire to be answered in writing is convenient for gathering information from a large number of people (542) in a brief period of time. However, such an approach fails to reveal the entire pattern of each person's reasoning when proposing consequences. To compensate for this limitation, we also used the six anecdotes as the stimuli for extended individual interviews with 20 additional respondents.

2

The People
Who Furnished Opinions

An important aim of our investigation was to discover the likely influence of different social environments on the consequences people suggest for wrongdoing and on the reasons they give in support of such consequences. The term *social environment* in this instance means the general cultural milieu of a group such as students living in a West Coast inner-city ghetto compared to ones in a small Hawaiian seacoast town. Thus, our analysis was at a general group level rather than at the level of intimate social relationships within individual families. By comparing the profiles of values expressed by groups from several cultural settings, we sought to estimate how social forces in those settings might affect people's judgments of wrongdoers.

Our intention in this chapter is to offer a brief demographic portrait of the groups we studied, including characteristics of their social environments that we believed would be useful in speculating about the way the cultural milieu of their daily lives might affect the values they expressed in the six cases.

In the following description of the groups, we have substituted fictitious names for their cities and institutions in order to protect the anonymity of the respondents. The seven groups were drawn from (1) Polk-Metro Public High School, (2) San Pablo Parochial High School, (3) Northcoast University's teacher-education program, (4) Makai Public High School in Hawaii, (5) Pele Community College in Hawaii, and (6) two institutions in Saudi Arabia —True-Faith High School and the University of the Prophet.

POLK-METRO PUBLIC HIGH SCHOOL

Polk-Metro is located in the most poverty-ridden section of a very large city in the southwestern United States. The Latino population at the school has grown over the past 10 years and is now in the majority. The other major ethnic group served by the school is African-American, a group that, until the past decade, was in the majority. Such demographic shifts have caused tension within the student population, a tension that erupted into riots several times in the early 1990s.

Table 2-1

Ages and Grades of Polk-Metro Students
N = 132

Age	%	Grade Level	%
14 years =	10	9th =	17
15 years =	28	10th =	39
16 years =	36	11th =	30
17 years =	18	12th =	8
No data =	8	No data =	6

The school's rate of student dropouts has remained around 45% since the 1980s. Polk-Metro ranks at the bottom of the schools of Metro County in terms of standardized state test scores in mathematics and reading. The majority of the freshman and sophomore students are held back each year because they lack sufficient credits to pass on to the next grade. One quarter of the female students give birth to babies each year, and over 80% of the students' families receive government assistance in the form of Aid to Families with Dependent Children (AFDC).

As in many inner cities, gang violence has escalated, bringing with it a steadily rising homicide rate, the leading cause of death for African-American males in the community. Illicit drugs are accessible and are a focus of much of the gang activity. Such easily affordable and highly addictive drugs as *crack* (a derivative of cocaine) are widely available. The profits from drug sales can reach thousands of dollars a month, providing a strong impetus for students to join gangs.

The community in which Polk-Metro is located suffers from problems common to many inner cities in the United States. Infant mortality, communicable disease, and general morbidity and mortality rates are the highest of any community in the county. Further, the area has the lowest rate of immunization and the lowest per-capita number of medical doctors in Metro County. Because of constant violence in the Polk-Metro district—including drive-by shooting—many children show signs of post traumatic stress disorder (PTSD). Most students at the school report that they have experienced the violent death of someone they knew.

For the purpose of the present study, opinionnaires were administered by classroom teachers to two science classes and two social-studies classes. The median age of the 132 respondents (62% female, 38% male) was 16 years. The proportion of the sample at each age and grade level is given in Table 2-1.

SAN PABLO PAROCHIAL HIGH SCHOOL

San Pablo High is the only secondary school operated by a religious order in the West Coast city of Vista Verde, population 90,000. In ethnic composition, the residents are 89% white, 1% black, 1% American Indian, 1.5% Asian or Pacific Islander, and 7.5% other. Ten percent of the whites are of Latino origin, most of them from Mexico. Data on the educational attainment of 44,000 adults in Vista Verde show that 64% graduated from high school and 21% from college or beyond, whereas 15% have attended only elementary school (grades 0 through 8).

A survey of 37,000 people composing Vista Verde's civilian labor force shows (a) 27% in managerial and professional careers; (b) 31% in technical, sales, and administrative support occupations; (c) 11% in precision production, craft, and repair; (d) 11% in service activities; (e) 10% as operators, fabricators, and laborers; (f) 8% as self-employed; and (g) 2% in farming and fishing.

In terms of income, the portion of the population listed at the poverty level is 7%. Violent crimes committed in Vista Verde the previous year totaled 419.

San Pablo High has around 500 students enrolled in grades 9 through 12. Parents pay tuition of $2,000 per student. In marked contrast to Polk-Metro, San Pablo has an annual dropout rate of only 2%, and no students are retained in the same grade at the end of the year for failing to earn enough credits to move ahead.

An informal study by a homeroom teacher provides a picture of the vocational plans and of parents' occupations among 92 third- and fourth-year San Pablo students. Table 2-2 compares the composition of the city's labor force, as reported above, with (a) the pattern of occupational hopes of San Pablo boys and

Table 2-2

Students' Expectations and Parents' Occupations
(in percentages)

Vocational Categories	Labor Force	Hoped-for Occupations		Parents' Occupations	
		Boys	Girls	Fathers	Mothers
Managers, Professionals	27	55	63	53	42
Technicians, Sales, Admin. Support	31	17	18	24	40
Service Occupations	11	17	8	6	8
Farming, Fishing, Forestry	2	10	9	2	
Precision Products, Craft, Repair	11			11	
Operators, Fabricators, Laborers	10	11	2	4	
Self Employment Activities	8				3
Housewives without Another Job					7

girls for 10 years in the future and (b) the current occupations of San Pablo students' fathers and mothers. In the table, parents who owned small businesses that they themselves operated are listed under "Managers, Professionals" rather than under "Self-Employment Activities." It is apparent from the table that not only did most San Pablo students come from families in the upper echelons of the occupational hierarchy, but a high proportion wished also to be in occupations ten years hence that were white-collar activities. In their predictions of the future, most of the students expected to be married (girls = 100%, boys = 75%) and to have one or two children (girls = 82%, boys = 72%). Nearly all of the San Pablo students currently lived with both a mother and a father. In contrast, many Polk-Metro students resided with only one parent, with members of their extended families, or with friends.

The great majority of San Pablo students were from families whose religion was Roman Catholicism. The remainder of the students were from families that were not practicing Catholics but that wanted their children to attend a school that fostered Christian morality and disciplined study.

San Pablo students are generally law abiding. Since the school is a private institution, students whose behavior or academic performance is unacceptable can readily be expelled without the school's administrators facing legal action. However, because school officials wish to keep enrollment figures up, they do occasionally blink at illegal behavior, so long as it does not obviously disturb the school's operation. For instance, students who are known users of drugs and alcohol are neither dismissed nor disciplined by the San Pablo faculty, but selling drugs on the school premises or attacking a teacher would result in immediate dismissal.

The average age of the 166 San Pablo students (58% female, 42% male) who participated in our study was 16.5 years. Their ages ranged from 16 to 18 years, with 92% of the group in the 16 to 17 bracket. They were enrolled in grades 10 through 12. Opinionnaires that students filled out for the present study were completed during a regular class period.

NORTHCOAST UNIVERSITY

Northcoast is a state university located in the small oceanside town of Timber in the lower Pacific Northwest. Because the area is remote from cities of any size, the university tends to attract students who are considered more adventurous and self-reliant than usual and whose homes are, on the average, 500 miles away. The school's surrounding environment is particularly appealing to students in science and natural-resources programs that feature curricula involving wildlife, forestry, and range management. Over the past decade the university has also increased its strength in the fine arts, business, and humanities. The institution's enrollment has grown steadily over the last five years.

In terms of ethnic background, the 8,000 members of the student body at the time of the present study identified themselves as 75% white, 3.5% Hispanic, 2.5% American Indian, 2% black, and 2% Asian. (The remaining 15% did not report their ethnic status.)

The 63 Northcoast students participating in this study (51% female, 49% male) were currently enrolled in a teacher-preparation program. All had earlier earned a bachelor's degree in some special subject-matter field. They were now in the university's post-graduate program to receive a state credential authorizing them to teach in grades 7 through 12. In age, the respondents ranged from 22 to 48 years, with a median of 32 years. In ethnic background, 91% of the 63 were white, 6% Hispanic, 1% American Indian, 1% Asian-American, and 1% African-American. In religious affiliation, 39% reported that they subscribed to no formal denomination, 28% were Christian Protestants, 15% were Catholics, 2% were Jews, and 16% were of other faiths.

Many of the older students had already been engaged in an occupation and were now returning to school to seek a second or sometimes a third career. Some said they had become disillusioned with the business world and hence were turning to teaching as a way of working with young people and "touching the future."

MAKAI PUBLIC HIGH SCHOOL

Makai is a small seacoast town in the Hawaiian Islands. The community is primarily residential and small-plot agricultural (vegetables, flowers), along with a bit of commercial fishing. The area has been troubled by a high delinquency rate and is inhabited by a high percentage of long-term poor, many of whom receive government financial assistance.

The 31 students who contributed to the just-deserts study were presently enrolled in a summer session at Makai Public High School. They ranged in age from 13 to 17 years, with a median of 15 years. They were enrolled in grades 9 through 12. Twenty-five were in an English class. The dominant language of the community is a form of Hawaii Creole (pidgin) English; by attending summer school, the 25 were attempting to improve their command of a more "standard" form of English. The remaining 6 participants were girls in a cheer-leading program.

The families of the students, in terms of socioeconomic status, were about evenly split between blue-collar workers and people supported by public welfare. In ethnic background, the 31 students were 67% Hawaiian or part-Hawaiian, 15% Japanese, 9% Samoan, and 9% Filipino.

PELE COMMUNITY COLLEGE

Pele is a two-year junior college located on the outskirts of the largest urban center in the state of Hawaii. All 24 students (54% females, 46% males) who participated in the present study attended college part-time, chiefly in the evenings, after working at a full-time job during the daytime hours.

The 24 respondents ranged in age from 18 to 46 years, with a median of 25 years. In terms of their present occupations, 43% were technicians in the U.S. military forces, 38% were office workers, 14% held managerial positions, and 5% were in sales. In ethnic origin, 42% were white and 21% Japanese, while the remaining 37% (8 students) represented the following eight ethnic groups: American Indian, Samoan, Mexican-Chinese, Anglo-Japanese, Japanese-Hawaiian, Chinese-Hawaiian, Japanese-Hawaiian-German, and Filipino-Spanish-Chinese.

All 24 students had enrolled in the college to obtain a two-year associate-of-arts degree. Many wished subsequently to continue their education by later earning a bachelor's degree in a university. When asked about the highest grade in school their parents had completed, 20% reported that their father had finished college, 60% of the fathers had completed high school, and 20% had attended a junior high. As for their mothers, 30% had graduated from a four-year college, 50% had finished high school, and 20% had attended a junior high. Hence, most of the 24 Pele students had already surpassed their parents in the amount of formal education they had obtained.

SAUDI ARABIAN SECONDARY SCHOOL AND UNIVERSITY STUDENTS

The Kingdom of Saudi Arabia is an oil-rich Middle-East nation of 14 million people, 73% of whom live in urban areas. The country's principal tourist feature is the Islamic holy city of Mecca, visited each year by millions of Muslim pilgrims from other parts of the world.

The most potent determinant of the society's customs is the Islamic religion. Formal social relations are governed by Islamic law, which is founded on the faith's principal guidebook, the *Koran* (divine truth revealed to Mohammed in the seventh century A.D.), and on the *Hadith* (collected sayings and deeds of Mohammed and his companions). These documents and interpretations of them by Islamic scholars define proper and improper behavior as well as consequences appropriate to both correct behavior and wrongdoing.

The 126 Saudi Arabian students who participated in the present study attended school in one of the nation's major cities. The sample included 44 high school students (22 females, 22 males) and 82 university students (41 females, 41 males). The average age of the secondary-school sample was 18 years and of the university sample 22 years. All were well steeped in Muslim rules of conduct by dint of their schooling, their home training, and their participation in Islamic religious life. All could be expected to know the types of sanctions typically imposed under Islam for various kinds of wrongdoing.

In Saudi Arabia, the opinionnaire survey was conducted in high school and university classes. Students were asked to indicate the consequences they would propose in the opinionnaire's six cases. Although they were also provided the chance to describe the rationales supporting their choices, almost none availed themselves of this opportunity.

OTHER PARTICIPANTS

Not only were consequence proposals collected by means of printed opinionnaires from the 542 members of the above groups, but the responses of an additional 20 individuals were gathered through direct interviews. Information from the opinionnaires was used for generating the components of the taxonomy and for comparing the six subgroups with each other. Information from the interviews was used for revealing differences among individuals in their overt moral-reasoning styles. The 11 females and 9 males who were interviewed ranged in age from 9 to 65. They came from a variety of California communities. Some lived in a large metropolitan area, whereas others were from small towns and rural areas.

CONCLUSION

The foregoing descriptive profiles of the six groups who filled out opinionnaires have been intended to provide some basis for speculating about causes that may underlie intergroup similarities and differences that could be revealed in intergroup comparisons. The principal demographic features we use in Part III for pursuing this second purpose are summarized in Table 2-3. They include (1) age, (2) amount of schooling, (3) socioeconomic status, (4) the law-abiding quality of the environment in terms of the amount of crime in the immediate society, and (5) religious affiliation.

As Table 2-3 indicates, we devised a method for producing a crude rating of the groups on three of the demographic features—economic status, the crime level of the social environment, and the extent of homogeneity in religious affiliation.

Both economic status and crime level were rated on five-point scales that extended from *low* through *medium-low*, *medium*, *medium-high*, to *high*. Thus, the inner-city Polk-Metro group was judged low in economic status because of the poverty condition of its surrounding neighborhood. The group was rated high on crime level because of the extreme incidence of homicides, gang-related crimes, and drug sales that plague the community. In contrast, the Saudi Arabians were rated high on economic status for the relatively high family income level of their oil-rich country ($41,118 annually at an average family size of 6.6 persons). The Saudi Arabians were ranked low on crime because of the strict policing of their society as guided by Islamic law. Similar types of

Table 2-3

Demographic Features of Six Groups of Respondents

Group's Title	N	Median Age	School Grade	Economic Status
Polk-Metro High	132	16	9-12	Low
San Pablo High	166	16.5	10-12	Medium-High
Northcoast U.	63	32	17	Medium-Low
Makai-Hawaii High	32	15	9-12	Medium-Low
Pele C. C.	24	25	13-14	Medium
Saudi Arabians	126	20	10-16	High

Group's Title	Crime Level	Religious Homogeneity	Ethnic Homogeneity
Polk-Metro	High	?	Divided
San Pablo	Low	Strong	Strong
Northcoast U.	Low	Mixed	Mixed
Makai-Hawaii High	Medium-High	?	Mixed
Pele C. C.	Medium-High	?	Mixed
Saudi Arabians	Low	Strong	Strong

indicators were used for placing the other four groups on the economic-status and crime-level scales.

Patterns of religious affiliation were rated on a three-level scale that was intended to reflect homogeneity of belief—*strong* homogeneity, affiliation *divided* between two or three main denominations, or *mixed* affiliation that was spread across a variety of belief systems. A rating of *strong* was applied to the Saudi Arabians, because all were Muslims. A similar rating was applied to the students of San Pablo High, since they attended a denominational school that included Catholic religious instruction in its curriculum. The label *mixed* was applied to the Northcoast University group because its membership was composed of nonreligious individuals and ones that subscribed to a diversity of religious assemblages. No information was available about religious preferences in the Polk-Metro, Makai, and Pele Community College samples.

Estimates of ethnic homogeneity were also reported by means of a crude three-level structure that included *strong* (over 85% of a single ethnic designation), *divided* (two or three ethnic types), and *mixed* (more than three ethnic types represented).

In the interpretation of the survey results in Part III, the contents of Table 2-3 will be used for speculating about how the six features of the table might help explain the patterns of responses of the groups that proposed consequences for offenders in the six cases of wrongdoing.

Part II

The Taxonomy of Rationales to Support Proposed Consequences

As noted in the first chapter, one of our prime goals in conducting the study was to collect material to use in devising a system for classifying the types of reasons people advance in defense of the consequences they recommend for wrongdoers. The purpose of Part II is to describe the taxonomy we derived from analyzing 542 respondents' expressed opinions from written opinionnaires and 20 from interviews. Throughout the description we include occasional references to the historical and philosophical backgrounds of the items in the system.

In preparation for the detailed narration, we first explain the method by which we generated the taxonomy.

THE METHOD OF CONSTRUCTING THE TAXONOMY

We began with no preconceived organizational categories into which we thought people's rationales would fit. In other words, we chose to be led by the data, extracting categories inductively by listing the respondents' answers from the opinionnaires.

As a first step, answers that were either identical or seemed clearly an alternate phrasing of the same idea were combined as one item in the list. For example, such responses as "Make the person suffer for the offense" and "The person should feel what it's like to be hurt" formed a single item. Even with such combining of answers, the list was very long, extending to more than 200 items. In effect, although respondents were reacting to only six moral incidents (three pairs), the participants provided a great diversity of moral-value rationales.

As a next step, items that appeared similar in intent were conceived to form a cluster, and a word or phrase was created to reflect the apparent essence of that cluster. To illustrate, the two responses *"She was too young to know better"* and *"In the society he comes from, what he did is not considered improper"* were both placed in a category entitled *Awareness of Right and Wrong.*

Finally, the labeled clusters were cast into five major groupings that appeared to represent broader generalizations. For instance, clusters labeled *Prevent*

Future Offenses by the Actor, *Deter Others from Misconduct,* and *Wreak Revenge* were collected under the title <u>*The Purpose of the Consequences*</u>. This process resulted in categories labeled (1) moral values, (2) purpose, (3) conception of causality, (4) consequence feasibility, and (5) agent qualifications.

In summary, our inspection of respondents' answers led us to offer the following basic framework for the taxonomy.

The consequences people recommend for wrongdoing are the product of a pattern of thought which
Usually includes:
Moral Values—A set of values composed of moral principles and their qualifying conditions.
The Purpose of Consequences—A conviction about the function the consequence is intended to perform.
Occasionally includes:
Conceptions of Causality—Beliefs about causation in the sense of what caused the wrongdoing and/or why the recommended consequence would likely accomplish its purpose.
Consequence Feasibility—An estimate of how feasibly a suggested consequence can be implemented.
Agent Qualifications—A belief about which individuals or agencies have the right and responsibility to assign consequences for wrongdoing.

We are thus suggesting that such a five-element scheme is useful for deriving a well-informed interpretation (a) of why people think their recommended consequences are just and practicable and (b) of how the beliefs of one individual or one group compare with those of another.

Specific kinds of decisions that we made at various steps in the process of assigning responses to the five categories and to their sublevels are identified at appropriate stages of Chapters 3, 4, and 5.

Before explaining the taxonomy, we should alert readers to an important limitation of the opinionnaire approach for yielding complete data about the five topics. When respondents filled out the opinionnaires, none of them supplied information about more than two or three of the categories. All respondents cited a consequence, and virtually all reflected moral values in their supporting rationales. However, only certain respondents offered an estimate of the cause of the misconduct, whereas others suggested a purpose the consequence should serve, and still others cited feasibility considerations. Therefore, using such an opinionnaire to collect people's beliefs enabled us to gather information from a large sampling of respondents within a relatively brief period of time, but it did not elicit answers from every respondent about all five of the taxonomy's major classes. Therefore, to supplement the opinionnaire survey, we also conducted an interview study with 20 people, focusing their attention specifically on all five categories. By this means we were able to learn something about the patterning the five factors can assume in the belief systems of different individuals. The results of the interview part of our investigation are given in Chapter 10.

The three chapters that make up Part II describe in detail our proposed method of ordering consequences. Chapter 3 explains the most detailed division, *Moral Values*. Chapter 4 describes the next two categories, *The Purpose of Consequences* and *Conceptions of Causality*. Chapter 5 focuses on the last two, *Consequence Feasibility* and *Agent Qualifications*.

In presenting a division, we first note the way items within that set are organized, then describe why we adopted such a structure. We next list the separate items, each identified by a title plus a short definition, by an occasional comment about the item's historical or theoretical background, and by examples of people's remarks that appear to be instances of that item.

A SCHEME FOR ORGANIZING CONSEQUENCES

As a foundation for inspecting the taxonomy's elements in Chapters 3, 4, and 5, we close this introduction with a brief review of three ways that proposed consequences of behavior have been categorized over the years, and we identify which of these we used with the taxonomy. The three patterns of categories are labeled the *Severity-Desirability Scale*, the *After-Effect Perspective*, and the *Consequence Types*.

Severity-Desirability Scale

This first method of arranging consequences involves locating them along a scale that extends from very severe punishment at one end to very desirable reward at the other. Criminal law typically implies such a scale by distinguishing levels of crimes (and the severity of their consequences) with such terms as *felony, misdemeanor*, and *violation*. Murder and grand theft (theft involving large amounts of money) are felonies, minor shoplifting and petty theft (small amounts of money) are misdemeanors, while jaywalking and parking in a loading zone are violations.

From the perspective of a recipient of a consequence, the meaning of this scale is more precise if the qualifying word *presumed* is added to the label, resulting in a dimension called *the presumed severity of punishment and presumed desirability of reward*. This is because someone who proposes a sanction is only guessing that the recipient of the sanction will interpret it to have the same meaning as that imagined by the proposer. So from the existential viewpoint of a wrongdoer, an intended act of punishment serves to punish only to the degree that the wrongdoer accepts the act as punishment. Likewise, an intended reward only has the effect of a reward to the degree that its recipient interprets the event as pleasurable.

Not only may there be a discrepancy between where on the scale a sanction-proposer and a recipient locate a given consequence, but one proposer can differ from another on how severe or desirable a consequence will be. This point became obvious in our opinionnaire survey, particularly in the case of the Nazi major who had carried out the slaying of Yugoslav partisans and later became a drug dealer in South America. One respondent wrote: "He deserves the worst punishment, death." Another wrote: "Killing is too good for him. He shouldn't get off that easy. Put him in prison at hard labor for life so he can suffer."

Likewise, in the case of the motorist who drove after drinking, one participant suggested: "Taking away his driver's license will be a lot more painful than just paying a fine and the women's medical expenses." A second participant wrote: "He could still drive without a license. Make him pay a big fine."

Aftereffect Perspective

The psychological school of behaviorism has popularized a way of interpreting consequences that focuses on how various kinds of sanctions influence a person's future behavior (Skinner, 1969, 1974).

Two foundational assumptions of behaviorist theory are that (a) each act a person performs is followed by one or more consequences and (b) those consequences determine how likely the person will act the same way when in similar stimulus situations in the future. Thus, from a behaviorist point of view, consequences are categorized in terms of whether their aftereffects have been to increase or to decrease the future incidence of a given action.

Key words in the behaviorist lexicon are *reinforcement, nonreinforcement, punishment,* and *extinction.* Any consequence that results in the increased use of an action in the future is considered to be a reinforcer. Consequences followed by a reduction of an action in the future are examples of nonreinforcement or punishment. Whenever, as the result of consequences, an action is completely eliminated from future behavior, it is said to be extinguished.

From the viewpoint of behaviorism, wrongdoing is reduced or eliminated by consequences that are nonreinforcing or punishing.

Throughout the following chapters, the term *aversive consequences* refers to sanctions an individual incurs which that individual interprets as punishment (unwanted and undesirable outcomes) or which are intended to be punitive by those who propose them. Proposers of consequences can differ in their estimate of how aversive a given consequence will be in the eyes of an offender. As one of the respondents in our study commented, "For a homeless guy, going to jail ain't all that bad."

Consequence Types

Our third option for organizing consequences involves constructing a typology within which sanctions can be situated. The approach we illustrate below is composed of two general varieties of consequences—ones involving punishment or reward and ones intended as support activities rather than as punishment or reward.

Under the punishment/reward category, punishments are placed in the left column and rewards in the right. Both the punishments and the rewards are pictured from the viewpoint of those who assign consequences rather than those who are recipients. Each form of consequence is described in terms of the observable acts and objects it entails. The seven types of sanctions concern physical treatment, property, rights and privileges, labor, training, verbal response in private or in public, and indeterminate consequences. Within the support-activity category, three kinds of consequences are identified—material, psychological, and instructional. A final category is that of imposing no sanctions or support activities at all—the wrongdoer is simply set free.

In some cases, the punishment or support activity is not aimed at the wrongdoers themselves but, rather, at their caretakers, such as the parents of a delinquent child. Some respondents in the present study suggested that the parents of the boy who stole the car radio should be required to participate in family-counseling sessions and to pay the injured police officer's hospital costs.

Category 1: Punishment/Reward

Forms of Punishment   Forms of Reward

Physical Treatment

Physical Harm. Kinds of physical harm can extend from the most drastic—torture and death—to the extremely mild, such as a modest slap on the behind or a slight pinch on the arm. During the twentieth century the incidence and severity of physical punishment have diminished in comparison to their use in earlier times. The trend, particularly in Western societies, has been to substitute other consequences for what have been labeled "cruel and inhuman" physical treatment of wrongdoers. However, in many parts of the world, including the United States, people convicted of such crimes as murder, rape, and treason are still executed. In a few societies, such punishments as flogging, stoning, and amputating the hands of thieves continue in use. Slapping and spanking are still common methods employed by parents and teachers as disciplinary measures.

Physical Enhancement. Providing consequences that improve an individual's appearance, strength, agility, or good health can qualify as physical rewards. Examples can include giving a person a membership in a health and fitness club or paying for someone's treatments at a beauty salon.

Property

Forfeiture of Property. The most common punishment meted out in both criminal and civil court cases is that of fining the transgressor an amount of money. However, money is not the only kind of property that may be forfeited. Objects used in committing misdeeds may be confiscated, as when guns used in robberies or automobiles used in illicit drug trafficking are seized by the authorities. As another variety of punishment, the transgressor may be required to

Provision of Property. For behaving in virtuous ways, people can be rewarded with prizes and gifts.

pay the cost of the damaged property. To
punish a youth for misbehavior, parents may
take away the youngster's favorite toy or a
cherished garment.

Rights and Privileges

In the present context, the words *rights* and *privileges* are invested with particular
meanings.

A *right* is defined as an opportunity to which an individual is entitled simply
by virtue of being a member·of the group to which that right applies. The
group that deserves this opportunity is typically identified by an adjective accom-
panying the word *right.* Thus, a *human right* is an advantage or opportunity
belonging to all *Homo Sapiens. Children's rights* are entitlements that apply to
those *Homo Sapiens* below a specified age level. *Citizens' rights* are accorded
everyone who qualifies for citizenship in a given society. *Prisoners' rights* are
due those incarcerated for wrongdoing (Ray & Tarrow, 1987, p. 5).

In contrast, the term *privileges* is used to mean advantages people have earned
by their individual behavior, rather than simply by their membership in a defined
group. Consequently, a 13-year-old girl has the right to expect food and shelter
from her parents, simply because she is a minor ward. But she does not have the
right to stay out until two o'clock in the morning. Staying out late qualifies as
a privilege she earns by responsible behavior—or by managing to intimidate her
parents into granting the privilege. Likewise, a 16-year-old boy has the right to
apply for a driver's license simply because he has entered the 16-year age-group.
However, he does not have a right to receive a driver's license. That is a
privilege he must earn by demonstrating the ability to drive safely.

Forms of Punishment

Forfeiture of Rights or Privileges. Oftentimes
the penalty imposed for misdeeds consists
of the removal of rights or privileges that the
transgressor previously enjoyed. As the most
extreme application of this kind of sanction,
the rights to life, liberty, and the pursuit of
happiness that are included in the U.S. Consti-
tution are all forfeited in cases of criminals
sentenced to death. Certain rights of citizenship, such as the opportunity to vote in public
elections, can be revoked for people convicted
of felonious crimes. Imprisonment denies an
individual the right of free movement, the
choice of companions, and normal employment.

The removal of privileges is a technique
commonly used with children and adolescents.
Parents may reduce the amount of time that a
disobedient son is allowed to watch television,

Forms of Reward

*Provision of Privileges and
Opportunities.* For virtuous
behavior, people are often rewarded with out-of-the-ordi-
nary opportunities, such as
the chance to engage in valued
social events, to mingle with
people of prestige and influence, or to win membership
or office in attractive organizations.

a teacher may keep a girl in the classroom at recess time to complete unfinished homework, and a scoutmaster may withhold from recalcitrant troop members the opportunity to go camping.

Placing an individual on probation restricts the person's right to free movement. Probation typically means that the wrongdoer is kept under special surveillance so as to discourage future misbehavior.

Boycott is a special form of removing rights or privileges. It consists of dissuading people from using the services or products of the person or organization against whom punishment is directed.

The obverse of boycotting is that of persuading others to adopt the products or services of a virtuous individual or organization.

Labor

Required Labor. For lawbreaking, required labor can involve heavy physical strain, such as breaking up rocks in a quarry or working on a road-construction gang. It can consist of mental effort, as in the social-service activity of teaching those who are functionally illiterate to read and write. At home a child may be assigned household chores as a sanction for disobedience. A common method of punishment in schools is that of assigning extra homework to students who misbehave. The imposed labor sometimes takes the form of a socially acceptable activity through which the transgressor can vent his or her anger and frustration, as may be true of physical labor.

Improved Work Opportunities or Relief from Labor. As a reward, people may be relieved of work, as occurs when an employee is allowed extra vacation time or a pupil is exempt from a school assignment. In other cases the reward takes the form of a chance to pursue a desirable type of work not available in the past. A laborer may be advanced to the post of foreman. A student may be given the chance to join the staff of the school newspaper.

Verbal Response in Private or in Public

Verbal Abuse—Private. A reprimand in either oral or written form is often administered to wrongdoers. The scolding can range from mild criticism to extremely harsh abuse. It is, however, administered in private, so only the transgressor is witness to the rebuke.

A second form of verbal response consists of requiring the offender to apologize to the people who were the objects of the wrongdoing.

Verbal Praise—Private. An individual is personally lauded in oral or written form for virtuous behavior. The event is not directly witnessed by others.

Exposure and Condemnation. A wrongdoer is publicly censured. The fact that others witness the event means that the recipient of the criticism can suffer public disgrace. The event

Acclaim and Commendation. Public recognition of morally approved acts can result from open oral praise of students in

may involve public exposure of a misdeed that the wrongdoer wished to keep secret, or it may consist of condemning an act that others knew about but had not regarded as a serious fault. The condemnation may be only temporary, as when a teacher criticizes a student in front of classmates; or it may be permanent, as with a written report of a crime that remains in public records for an extended period of time. The exposure of misdeeds in the public press tends to be permanent, since they are widely publicized and the accounts are easily retrieved in the future by interested parties.

the classroom, from the public award of certificates to employees or community members, and the like. Virtuous acts are often revealed to the public through news media.

As another possibility, the wrongdoer may be required to make a public confession of the misdeed or a public apology for the offense.

Indeterminate Consequences

Sometimes people suggest that sanctions be imposed, but they fail to specify the nature of the sanctions. This can happen when people cannot decide what sort of consequence is most suitable. In other cases, they assume that the decision rests with some authoritative body— "punishment as specified by law" or "what the jury or judge decides."

Category 2: Support Activities

Material Support

Goods and Services. The transgressor or the transgressor's caretaker may be furnished material goods, such as money, food, shelter, clothing, school supplies, occupational tools, and the like. The support may consist of such services as child-care provisions or transportation to school or work.

Psychological Support

Counseling. Wrongdoing is often seen as resulting from a breakdown of the transgressor's self-control and ability to cope with life's difficulties in a socially acceptable manner. Psychological counseling can be recommended as a consequence intended to rebuild the wrongdoer's impaired coping skills. The counseling may be combined with medical treatment, such as providing lithium for an individual diagnosed as suffering from manic depression or furnishing a drug addict a substance intended to wean him or her away from harmful drugs.

Instructional Support

Improving Skills and Knowledge. Often allied with psychological support are consequences that involve teaching a wrongdoer or a caretaker new skills, new knowledge, new values, or new attitudes. Such is the case when an alcoholic is required to attend Alcoholics Anonymous sessions, when a learning disabled child is provided special reading lessons to help remedy dyslexia, when a parent is ordered to follow a course in child-raising practices, or when prison inmates are obliged to learn a trade in a prison vocational training program.

Category 3: No Sanctions or Support Activities

Sometimes people accused of wrongdoing are simply set free without punishment, treatment, or support. This can occur under a variety of conditions, such as an offender is not held responsible for the misdeed ("It wasn't his fault" or "She didn't mean to do it"), the person committed the offense under duress ("They probably would have killed him if he didn't do what they said"), or a first-time offender is judged to deserve a second chance ("He's just a kid without much experience, and he really didn't know how much trouble it would cause, so he should only be warned this time. If he does it again, then he should be sent to juvenile hall").

CONCLUSION

In the foregoing discussion we have described three ways of categorizing consequences for wrongdoing. In the remainder of this book, we depend chiefly on the third method, which divides consequences into a variety of types. We prefer the third option because it is more readily applied than the first two in analyzing data from our opinionnaires and interviews.

The problem with the first approach is that it requires judgments about the individually perceived severity and desirability of different consequences. We lack information about the proper placement on a severity-desirability scale of any particular consequence from the viewpoint of either the proposer of the sanction or the intended recipient. Our personal estimate of how harsh or how attractive a consequence might be for an individual cannot be regarded as a valid reflection of how others would interpret that same consequence.

The difficulty with the second approach—the aftereffect perspective—is that there is no proper way to categorize a consequence as a reinforcer or nonreinforcer until we have information about how the wrongdoer behaves on subsequent occasions. In our study, we have information about kinds of sanctions recommended by opinionnaire and interview respondents, but obviously we know nothing about the subsequent behavior of the hypothetical characters in the incidents.

Thus, we are left with the third option—types of consequences that can be categorized on the basis of the kinds of acts they would involve.

Finally, we should explain that we do not consider the taxonomy in Part II to be a finished product. We see it as only a beginning. It needs to be further refined and expanded. We believe such refinement and extension might best be accomplished by researchers confronting respondents with additional cases of wrongdoing that involve moral principles and life conditions other than those included in our half-dozen cases.

3

Moral Values:
Principles and Conditions

A key assumption underlying our study of just deserts is that people's recommendations about consequences for wrongdoing will frequently reflect the values on which they base their proposals. Our approach to identifying such values is described in the following pages.

In Chapter 1 we argued that the analysis of moral values can profitably be viewed in terms of both *principles* and *conditions*.

Principles are *unqualified statements of belief*, meaning that the application of the principle to an event in life is not influenced by circumstances particular to the people, time, or place involved in the event. Examples of unqualified statements found in the biblical ten commandments (*Holy Bible*, 1611, Exodus, chap. 20) are: do not have any gods other than Jehovah; do not carve idols of gods; never use God's name lightly as in cursing; do not work on the Sabbath day; honor your parents; and do not kill, steal, lie about others, commit adultery, or yearn for your neighbors' possessions. Examples of principles from Gert's (1970) moral rules are: don't kill, don't cause pain, don't disable, don't deprive others of freedom or opportunity, don't deprive others of pleasure, don't deceive, keep your promise, don't cheat, obey the law, and do your duty.

Conditions are *characteristics of a particular event in life that influence the moral significance of that event*. In the present context the expression *moral significance* refers to such matters as estimating causes of the event, assigning blame or credit to people involved in the incident, and proposing consequences to be experienced by participants in the event. Our conviction is that rarely, if ever, does anyone apply a moral principle in an identical manner in all situations. We contend that conditions probably always affect the application of moral principles. Hence, in order to understand people's modes of moral reasoning, we need to identify not only the principles they hold but also the patterning of conditions they employ when applying principles to events involving morality. Therefore, the two main categories we propose under this first division are those of principles and conditions.

When we had completed a first draft of this moral-values chapter, we recognized that, for the purpose of constructing a generally useful taxonomy, our listing of both principles and conditions was constrained by the fact that respondents had offered opinions about only six cases of wrongdoing. It was obvious that a good many other principles and conditions than those reflected in the six anecdotes would be found in people's conceptions of moral values. For example, our cases failed to reveal values people could apply in cases of deceit, rape, forgery, arson, intimidation, exploitation, and more. Thus, in order to extend the moral-values section beyond the items extracted from responses to the six cases, we expanded the lists of principles and conditions by analyzing instances of wrongdoing reported in the daily news media over a period of one month. In the following lists, to indicate which principles and values were based on each of the two sources (opinionnaires and news media), we placed an asterisk (*) at the end of those items founded solely on the survey of news media. Items based on our opinionnaire survey and interviews are not followed by an asterisk.

MORAL PRINCIPLES

Principles are generalizations that define characteristics of the morally good or proper life. More precisely, principles identify (a) responsibilities or obligations that people should assume in their treatment of others or (b) the rights that a person deserves to enjoy or (c) rules governing the conduct of society so as to promote the obligations and rights.

In the following list, principles have been organized in four sets that are displayed in two parallel columns. The left column states the moral value in a positive form—what a person *should* do. The right column offers the same value in a negative form—what a person *should not* do. The sets are labeled (1) general societal obligations, (2) affective regard for others, (3) personal rights, and (4) sexual relations. In every set, a brief introductory comment about the nature of the set is followed by the individual principles. Each principle is labeled, defined, and accompanied by examples of people's remarks which appear to reveal the application of that value to moral events. Under principles that are not accompanied by an asterisk, the quoted remarks are ones taken from the opinionnaires and interviews collected in the present study. Quotations listed under principles that are identified with an asterisk have been drawn from comments in the daily news media rather than from opinionnaires or interviews.

General Societal Obligations The 10 items in this group focus on values that contribute to an orderly, predictable, and just society. The first five are basic rules for the systematic conduct of a moral society. The sixth (reward for righteousness) and seventh (reformation of misbehavior) propose methods for ensuring that people learn to abide by moral principles. The eighth (obedience to authority) assumes the need for a hierarchy of authority if unified social action is to result. The ninth (evenhanded justice) is intended to promote equity in the treatment of the society's members. The final principle (conservation) has always been a concern in cultures suffering a scarcity of resources, but in recent times it has achieved a new significance within affluent, wasteful cultures that are newly being confronted with imminent shortages of goods and with threats of environmental pollution. Conservation measures are intended to foster the continued stability of the society by reducing social conflicts over diminishing resources.

Virtues to Be Encouraged

Transgressions to Be Avoided

Respect for Right and Morality: Everyone should abide by moral principles and support others' actions that represent the right thing to do.
   "Whether or not the law requires restitution, paying the injured boy's medical bills is the right thing to do."

Disregard or Disdain for Right and Morality: No one should disregard or scorn moral principles.
   "No matter if the girl is from a poor home, what she did is wrong."

(Note: This value not only includes formal laws and regulations that are based on moral precepts but also encompasses acts bearing on morality that are not covered by formal rules. The interpretation of what constitutes *right* may differ from one group to another and from one individual to another.)

Protection of the Society: People should act in ways that protect the structure and operation of their society.
   "The society will be better off if the girl is put in a foster home and given love and guidance rather than just being locked up."

Destruction of the Society: No one should behave in ways that undermine the social order.
   "If people are allowed to act like that, the whole social system falls apart."

Respect for the Law: Everyone should obey formally constituted laws and should support the laws' implementation.
   "According to the law, the policeman did the right thing by arresting the boy."

Disregard or Disdain for the Law: No one should break formally constituted laws or hold the laws in contempt.
   "With selling drugs and using a weapon, the girl broke two laws."

(Note: This principle represents a subcategory under "Respect for Right and Morality" in that its focus is limited to formal rules, regulations, and laws, whether or not they accurately reflect an individual's conception of proper moral values.)

Responsibility: Everyone should fulfill those obligations that by custom are considered duties in keeping with the individual's stage of life or roles that he or she assumes in the society.
   "He should make restitution to the victim."

Irresponsibility: No one should avoid carrying out obligations incurred by the nature of one's role in life.
   "He should not be so immature in how he's handling his divorce."

(Note: Responsibility, as intended here, includes all types of obligation that people incur, either by unwritten custom or by formal agreement.)

Contractual Integrity: People who have freely agreed, in either written or oral form, to perform an action should faithfully carry out that commitment.
   "When you get a driver's license, you

Contractual Unreliability: People should never avoid performing actions that they have freely agreed to carry out.
   "He knew he shouldn't drive after

commit yourself to obey the traffic laws."   drinking, but he did it anyway."
(Note: Contractual integrity is the subcategory under "Responsibility" that
concerns formal agreements people enter into that involve the individual's
assuming obligations in return for certain privileges and rewards. Examples of such agreements are those made when people get married, are
provided a driver's license, obtain a permit to operate a business, are
certified to practice a profession, become an employee, open a bank
account, receive a credit card, and the like.)

Reward for Righteousness: All morally
correct behavior deserves to be rewarded.
  "The teacher did the right thing by
  stopping the girl from selling drugs,
  so he ought to be congratulated."

Punishment for Misdeeds: All acts
of wrongdoing should be punished.
  "He can't be allowed to get away
  without paying some price."

Reformation of Misbehavior: The proper
response to wrongdoing is to submit the
offender to a type of treatment that will
result in a reformation so he or she will
behave morally in the future.
  "If he's to straighten out his life, this boy
  needs the help of a loving family instead
  of a jail sentence."

Punishment of Misbehavior: Every
act of misbehavior should be retaliated with punishment.
  "People should not be let off the
  hook by escaping punishment."

(Note: *Treatment* and *punishment* can be intertwined in diverse ways. For
present purposes, *punishment* can be defined as the imposition of sanctions
intended to cause the recipient pain (physical or psychological); loss of
something valued; inconvenience; and/or such emotional reactions as fear,
guilt, and shame. *Treatment* can be defined as the provision of experiences
intended to alter a wrongdoer's behavior in socially desirable ways. Some
people recommend punishment solely as a device for gaining revenge, for
paying back the offender. Others, however, intend punishment to be a
treatment, with the pain and inconvenience suffered by the offender conceived
to be an effective deterrent to future misbehavior. This aim is reflected in such
comments as, "A year in jail will give him time to think about what he's done"
or "Having to pay a big fine should teach her a good lesson." Thus, when
someone recommends punishment as a sanction, we cannot judge whether the
sanction is intended as a treatment or a "pure punishment" unless we learn
what goal the recommender hopes the consequence will accomplish. In
Chapter 4, this issue of the purpose of consequences is discussed at length.)

Obedience to Authority: Everyone should
obey properly constituted authorities.
  "The colonel was in charge, so the major
  did the right thing by carrying out the
  colonel's orders."

Disobedience to Authority: No one
should disobey properly constituted
authorities.
  "The kid should have obeyed his
  parents."

Evenhanded Justice: Laws and regulations should be applied equally to
everyone. Opportunities to prosper
should be equally open to all.
  "The boy on the bike deserves to be

Privileged or Prejudicial Treatment:
No one should be treated in either a
privileged or a prejudicial manner in
the administration of laws and regulations and in the provision of

treated fairly. The woman should pay all his medical costs, just as if he had been at fault, he should have had to pay her expenses."

opportunities to prosper.
"Just because he's had a bad marriage doesn't mean that he shouldn't be punished like anybody else."
"Rich or poor, lawbreakers should all be treated the same."

Conservation: People should take only amounts of resources or goods that are necessary for the intended purpose. Whenever possible, waste materials should be recycled to produce new products.*
"Recycling paper saves the forests whose continued survival is crucial to the survival of humanity."

Wastefulness, Extravagance: People should not take more of any resources than is necessary for the intended purpose. Goods that can be recycled should not be discarded or left unused.*
"If people just keep throwing things away, the earth will become one enormous trash dump, unfit for habitation."

Affective Regard for Others The nine items listed below are closely related to the societal obligations proposed above, since the nine can influence the stability of the social order. However, we have located them in this separate section because they appear more specifically to represent emotional, empathetic relations between individuals and groups than do the general societal obligations.

Concern for Human Life—Physical: Everyone should protect others from physical harm and should seek to enhance their physical well-being.
"The teacher wasn't trying to hurt the girl. He was just trying to stop her from harming other kids by getting them on drugs."

Disregard for Human Life—Physical: No one should exploit or harm others physically.
"The colonel had all those Yugoslavs killed."

Concern for Human Life—Psychological: Everyone should protect others from intellectual and emotional harm and should seek to enhance their psychological well-being.
"The girl needs counseling so she can get her life in order. Sending her to detention won't help her do that."

Disregard for Human Life—Psychological: No one should exploit or damage others either mentally or emotionally.
"The boy must have felt terrible, with parents that threw him out on the street. They're the ones that ought to be punished."

Social Amity: Everyone should seek to maintain pleasant relations with others and to foster the group solidarity that supports the established social order.
"If the drunk driver is required to do some community service, he will be helping others and help make up for the trouble he caused."

Social Conflict, Social Disorder: No one should contribute to social conflict or to ill feeling within the group.
"Putting the girl in juvenile hall could cause her to hate people even more and then do more harm to others when she gets out."

Honesty: Everyone should tell the truth whenever the welfare of others is at stake.*
"The old saying that honesty is the best policy makes life far more dependable."

Deceit: No one should deceive others by lying or by deviously withholding the truth when the welfare of others is concerned.*
"The congressman was obviously lying, so he deserves to be put out of office."
"Advertisers who deceive the public need to be prosecuted."

Respect for Property: Everyone should protect others' right to hold and use property to which they have legal claim.
"It's the cops' job to see that people don't steal things from cars."

Stealing & Vandalism: No one should take or use others' property without their permission. No one should damage others' property.
"The teenager was ripping off somebody's car radio, and that's being a thief."

Loyalty, Faithfulness: Everyone should support in word and deed those people or causes to which duty or gratitude is owed.
"The major was just being faithful to the Nazi cause when he carried out the colonel's orders."

Disloyalty, Treachery: No one should fail to support in word and deed those people or causes to which duty or gratitude is owed.
"The boy's parents are at fault for dumping him out on the street instead of giving him the love and guidance that is their duty."

Gratitude: Everyone should express thanks for aid and support provided by others.*
"The girl who won the race thanked her mother for helping over the years."

Ingratitude: No one should fail to extend thanks for aid and support provided by others.*
"After his parents sacrificed to send him to college, he just criticized them for not buying him a car, too."

Respect for Parents: Everyone should show high regard for the opinions and wishes of one's parents.
"I think the girl was doing what her mother wanted—helping get money for the family."

Disrespect for Parents: No one should insult or defame his or her parents.
"He probably wouldn't obey his parents, and that's why they kicked him out."

Compassion, Altruism: Everyone should exhibit sympathy for, and offer aid to, people who suffer misfortune.
"She'd be helping the victim by paying his medical bills."
"She should compensate the people she injured."

Disdain, Coldheartedness: No one should ignore or scorn people who suffer misfortune.
"He saw the executions and did nothing to stop this madness, so he is an accomplice to the crime."

<u>Personal Rights</u> The six principles in this section focus on what individuals can expect from the society.

Self-Preservation, Self-Interest: All people deserve to fulfill their own needs; to protect themselves from physical, psychological, and social harm; and to enjoy as much happiness as possible.

"The Yugoslavs were doing the right thing by fighting the Germans in order to save their country."

"It was natural for the kid to hit the cop. He was just trying to defend himself."

Self-Destruction, Self-Denial: No one should carry out acts that will unduly damage himself or herself physically, psychologically, or socially.

"By drinking and then driving, he not only hurt others; he damaged himself, too, and that's stupid."

Self-Determination: All people, within their levels of ability, should be allowed to decide on the way they will live their lives, provided that (a) they do not unduly intrude on others' rights to lead their lives and (b) they bear their fair share of responsibility in caring for their own welfare and for that of the group.

"Since the colonel behaved himself while living in South America, he should be set free to live his life as he chooses."

Exploitation: No one should be forced to yield to the demands of others in ways that decrease the individual's self-perceived welfare, provided that the individual bears a fair share of responsibility in caring for his or her own welfare and the welfare of the group.

"Maybe the girl's mother forced her to go out and sell drugs, and now the girl ends up suffering for it."

Reasonable Punishment: People's right to humane treatment should be considered when sanctions for wrongdoing are applied.

"Putting him in prison for the rest of his life is good enough to teach him a lesson; I don't believe in killing even criminals."

Cruel or Unusual Punishment: No one should have to suffer cruel and unusual punishment.

"Some people would say the Nazi should be tortured, but I think that's inhuman."

Fair Opportunity: Everyone should have a fair chance to pursue occupational, social, and avocational activities suited to their stage of life and potential talents.

"If the teenage boy is kept in school and maybe gets a job, then he can make something worthwhile out of his life rather than sitting idly in juvenile hall."

Restricted Opportunity: No one should be prevented because of their social, economic, gender, or age status from pursuing activities suited to their stage of life and potential talents.

"Putting the drunk driver in jail might make him lose his job."

Right to a Productive Life: Each individual deserves the opportunity to pursue a productive life.

"If he is required to do community service, he can help make up for what he has done and feel that he's doing something good."

Forced Idleness or Misuse: No one should be required to waste his or her time in forced idleness or in activities considered unconstructive.

"Sending her to jail would prevent her from getting a job and making something of herself."

Right to Privacy: All people should be free from unwanted attention or intrusions into their lives.*

Uninvited Intrusion: No one should invade others' lives without their consent.*

"The singer should be allowed to lead his own life without being molested by his fans when he's not on the stage."

"The police shouldn't have searched her house without her permission or a search warrant."

Sexual Relations This final set represents a particular kind of relations between individuals. It also involves special concerns about how the sex-behavior principles that people adopt will affect the social order. Unlike such durable principles as honesty, responsibility, and contractual integrity, those governing sexual behavior have been undergoing rapid change in recent times. As a consequence, conflicting principles exist side-by-side within many societies, with one segment of the populace subscribing to one variety and other segments adopting opposing principles. To reflect this situation, the following list includes precepts that can be in conflict with each other. More traditional views from both Western and Eastern cultures appear earlier in the list, and more recent views are placed later.

Willing Participation: Sexual acts should involve the participation solely of freely consenting partners.*
"They were both adults and both wanted to make love, so it was okay."

Forced Participation: No one should, by either psychological or physical force, require sexual acts of another person.*
"He purposely got her drunk and then had sex with her when she really didn't want it at all."

Consentual Sexual Advances: Sexual attention and advances should occur only when both individuals express an interest in such behaviors. People in positions of authority should not force attention on another who is in a subordinate position.*
"They were coworkers, but it was okay for them to have a love affair, because it was they both said they wanted."

Imposed Sexual Advances: No one should make sexual advances or direct attention toward another in a sexual manner unless it is by mutual consent in an atmosphere free of coercion.*
"Just because he's her boss at work doesn't give him the right to touch her or tell sexy jokes."

(Note: The following three principles concern the question of what types of sexual partners are morally proper. Because societal standards of what constitutes proper versus improper partners have been undergoing revision in recent decades in many societies, there is currently no general consensus regarding a moral principle governing such issues. To reflect the transitional nature of the sex-partner standard, we have listed below three alternative versions labeled traditional, heterosexual, and bisexual.}

Proper Sexual Partners—Traditional: Sexual intercourse should be limited to couples of opposite sex who are married to each other.*

Improper Sexual Partners—Traditional: Sexual intercourse is immoral if it is between people not legitimately married to each other.*

"Even though professionally they had kept their own names so people thought they were still single, they were really a married couple, so they were doing nothing wrong by making love."

(Marriage between people of the same sex is illegitimate.) "Because what they did was adultery, they deserved the public disgrace they got."

Proper Sexual Partners—Heterosexual: Sexual intercourse should involve only a male with a female partner.*
"It was a woman and a man, not two men or two women, so what they did was quite all right."

Improper Sexual Partners—Heterosexual: Sexual intercourse between those of the same sex is immoral.*
"God's reason for creating people with sex urges was to populate the world, so homosexuality is contrary to God's law."

Proper Sexual Partners—Bisexual: Sexual intercourse should be limited to human adults (either of the opposite sex or of the same sex).*
"Two consenting people—that's the rule. It doesn't matter whether it's between a man and a woman or between a pair of the same sex."

Improper Sexual Partners—Bisexual: Sexual intercourse involving children or a nonhuman partner is immoral.*
"He imposed sex on a minor who was too young to give truly informed consent, and for that he deserves punishment to the fullest extent of the law."

Although the foregoing review of 30 principles falls far short of the total number of moral values to which people can subscribe, the list is sufficiently inclusive to accommodate the rationales offered by respondents who suggested consequences for wrongdoers in the present study. The list extends somewhat beyond the transgressions displayed in our six cases by drawing on instances of morality described in the news media over a period of one month.

We next consider circumstances that can influence the way people apply such principles to specific moral-decision incidents.

CONDITIONS AFFECTING THE APPLICATION OF PRINCIPLES

Like the moral principles, conditions are listed under a pair of columns. The left column describes circumstances that warrant *less serious* aversive consequences for wrongdoing, whereas the right describes conditions warranting *more serious* aversive sanctions. In the following list, the terms *actor, offender, transgressor,* and *wrongdoer* are used as synonyms to identify the person who has committed a misdeed. The conditions are ones influencing people's decisions about the proper level of severity of consequences for wrongdoing in light of circumstances obtaining in a particular moral event. All 44 of the conditions in the list were extracted from rationales offered by participants in our opinionnaire survey.

A separate class of conditions involves matters of *practicability*, meaning the feasibility of implementing a recommended sanction. This second class is located in Chapter 4 under *Consequence Feasibility.*

The following conditions are presented in eight clusters labeled: (1) character traits, (2) prior circumstances, (3) concurrent circumstances, (4) post-incident circumstances, (5) fair chance, (6) extent of damage, (7) legal considerations, and (8) value compatibility.

Conditions Warranting Less Severe Aversive Consequences	**Conditions Warranting More Severe Aversive Consequences**

<u>Character Traits</u> Such characteristics are assumed to be relatively permanent features of the offender's personality that surface on the occasion of a particular incident.

Good Character: The actor is generally a good person.
> "She's not a hard-core criminal, so she doesn't deserve to be jailed."

Bad Character: The actor is generally a bad person.
> "It was probably his fault that his wife divorced him."
> "A murderer is always a potential future murderer."

Absence of Malevolence: In committing the offense, the actor bore no ill will toward the recipient, so did not act out of animosity or malevolence.
> "She didn't really mean to hurt the the boy on the bike."

Malice: The actor committed the offense out of hatred or spite and with the desire to do harm.
> "He must have hated all Yugoslavs."

Redeeming Reason: The offender knew the rule or custom in question and violated it purposely, but only in order to comply with a conflicting but worthy value.
> "She was probably selling dope to help support her mother and sisters."

Inexcusable Violation: The actor was cognizant of the rule or custom and purposely violated it without any redeeming reason, such as to promote a laudable conflicting value.
> "The doctor explicitly told her not to drive when using the medication."

Knowledge of Right and Wrong: The person did not realize that the behavior violated a rule or custom, because the actor was either uninformed or was not in a rational mental state.
> "She was too young to know better."
> "The woman probably didn't understand the potency of the medicine."

Informed Violation: The person was aware of the rule or custom and purposely violated it without any redeeming reason.
> "Even though he was depressed, he still knew what he was doing when he drank and drove."

Role Suitability: The transgressor's behavior was in keeping with his or her role in life.
> "In wartime, a soldier's job is to kill the enemy."

Role Unsuitability: The offender's behavior was not in keeping with any legitimate, assigned role.
> "War does not mitigate the evil of the officer's crime."

<u>Prior Circumstances</u> These are conditions existing before the incident of wrongdoing. Such conditions may have contributed to the development of the personal traits noted above.

Societal Determinism: The actor should not be blamed, for he or she is simply a product of the society, so the society is responsible for the offense.

"Man is a reflection of society so is morally innocent."

"The boy is a victim of a system which doesn't care about kids."

Personal Determinism: The actor has a free will and carries responsibility for his or her own behavior and thus deserves the consequences warranted by such irresponsibility.

"Being homeless does not justify hitting someone with a pipe."

"The woman knew what the effects of the medicine might be."

Inadequate Social Support: The actor did not receive the personal/social support that would encourage law-abiding behavior (inadequate parental guidance, poor models of behavior, lack of reinforcement of good behavior).

"The root of the problem is that no one cares enough for her."

"This kid never had a chance to grow up right."

Adequate Social Support: The actor has had the kinds of personal/social support that would reasonably foster good behavior. Actors cannot blame their social background for their antisocial behavior.

"Being put out by his parents is still no excuse for violence."

Concurrent Circumstances Conditions surrounding the occasion of the offense are considered to be significant factors in judging the wrongdoer's culpability.

Accidental Violation: The actor was cognizant of the rule or custom but violated it unintentionally. It was simply an error, a kind of accident.

"Maybe the stop sign was hard to see, and that's why he missed it."

Intentional Violation: The actor was aware of the rule or custom and purposely violated it without any redeeming reason.

"She was intentionally driving under the influence of drugs."

"The boy chose to steal and attack the police officer."

Spontaneity: The transgression was unplanned, that is, committed on the spur of the moment and without careful thought about the results.

"The girl hadn't intended to stab the teacher. She was just scared when she got caught."

Premeditation: The action was planned ahead of time, with malice aforethought, so the actor knew the unfortunate consequences that would likely occur for recipients of the offense.

"She must have intended to stab somebody. Why else did she carry a knife?"

Emotional Surge: The offense was committed while the actor was incited by a surge of high emotion, such as fear, distress, or anger.

"The kid was startled when the cops grabbed him, so he just struck out."

Coldheartedness: The offense was committed when the actor was in a calculating mood, not stimulated by a sudden burst of emotion.

"The Nazi colonel carefully planned to kill all those Yugoslavs. It just wasn't done in the heat of battle."

Involuntary Loss of Inhibition: The person's psychological state reduced

Need to Abide by Inhibition: A person's psychological condition does

or eliminated inhibitions that normally could have restrained him or her from committing the misdeed.

> "The liquor was at fault. He wouldn't have hit the women's car if he had been sober."

Provocation (Warranted Retribution): The recipient of the offense had harmed the actor and thus invited retaliation.

> "The Yugoslavs had been fighting the Germans, so the Nazi officer was just fighting back."

Overpowering Personal Problems: The offender's personal problems understandably overwhelmed his or her self-control.

> "The girl has no father, and the family has no money, so she was peddling pot to survive."

Duress: The actor committed the offense at the command of another person.

> "If he had refused to supervise the executions, he would have been executed himself; so he had no choice."

Misperception: The transgressor innocently misperceived the moral-decision situation and thus thought there was no wrongdoing involved.

> "He may have been given false reasons for executing the people."

Reasonable Risk: The risk the actor took was reasonable, and it was just bad luck that it resulted in the offense.

> "He'd probably driven home after drinking before and never had any trouble, so he likely figured it was no big deal."

Unfavorable Physical Environment: Conditions of the physical environment contributed significantly to the offense.

> "If it was dark and the kid on the bike didn't have any lights, then the

not free that person from taking responsibility for his or her actions.

> "The doctor warned her not to drive when she was using the medicine, but she went ahead and did it anyway, so she deserves to be punished."

Innocent Recipient: The recipient of the offensive act had done nothing to the actor. The act was unprovoked.

> "The women were innocent victims of the drunk driver."

Personal Problems Inconsequential: The offender's personal problems do not justify such wrongdoing.

> "Being poor is no excuse for stabbing someone."
>
> "His marital difficulties do not excuse his drinking and driving."

Volition: The actor committed the offense of his or her own choice, not at the command of another person.

> "Nobody forced the boy to steal the car stereo. It was his own choice."

Nonplausible Claim of Misperception: The transgressor's claim of misinterpreting the moral-decision situation is unconvincing.*

> "He didn't consider it rape, because when she went out with him, he thought that meant she wanted to make love."

Unreasonable Risk: The actor showed bad judgment in taking risks that would likely lead to trouble.

> "The woman was stupid to take a chance on driving when she'd been told it was dangerous."

Physical Environment Insignificant: It is unlikely that conditions of the physical environment contributed to the offense.

> "If you can't even see a stop sign or a

woman maybe couldn't see him."

car coming on the cross street, you're really in a bad way."

Age Warrants Compassion: The transgressor is either too young or too old to deserve strict sanctions.
"At age 13 the boy can't be held fully responsible for the legal consequences of his act."

Age Irrelevant: The age of the transgressor should have no bearing on the sanctions imposed.
"He was old enough to make a responsible decision."

Right to Act: In order to take action that affects the welfare of others, a person needs to have proper authority or a legitimate reason to do so.
"In wartime the officer in charge has the right to give orders to kill."

Absence of Right to Act: No one should take action that affects the welfare of others without proper authority or a legitimate reason to do so.
"Nobody has the right to kill. Deciding when someone should die is nobody's responsibility but God's."

Excusable Behavior: What seems to be improper behavior can be excused if the circumstances in the case are sufficiently demanding.
"The girl was just defending herself. If the teacher hadn't grabbed her, he wouldn't have been hurt."

Inexcusable Behavior: Unless there are legitimate extenuating circumstances, misdeeds cannot be excused.
"There is no excuse for driving after drinking."

Suspension of Rules: The usual rules governing moral behavior do not apply in this particular context.
"It was wartime, and killing is what war is all about, so the man should not be punished for killing."

Nonsuspension of Rules: The usual standards of moral behavior continue to apply in this particular context.
"Murder is murder in any situation. The the fact that a war was going on makes no difference."

Solely an Accomplice: The offender played only a minor, supporting role in committing the misdeed.
"Killing the Yugoslavs wasn't the major's idea. He was just carrying out orders."

Direct Perpetrator: The offender was a direct perpetrator of the transgression.
"The major was just as much to blame as the colonel. When you purposely contribute to a crime, you deserve the full penalty."

Post-Incident Circumstances   People who propose consequences often include in their consideration certain conditions that occur between the time of the misdeed and the time the offender is caught or sentenced. In the following list, the first item is an overall judgment regarding whether post-incident circumstances should be considered at all when imposing consequences. The remaining items are specific conditions that may be weighed in determining consequences.

Later Events Significant: Events and conditions that occurred after the time of the offense should be considered when sanctions are proposed.

Later Events Inconsequential: Events and conditions subsequent to the time of the wrongdoing should have no bearing on the sanctions proposed for

"It's important to know how the person has responded after doing something wrong."

the transgression.

"What the Nazi officer did in South America is irrelevant."

Mature Reaction: The offender is responding to his or her situation in a mature, socially constructive manner.
  "The Nazi colonel has been a law-abiding citizen since the war."

Immature Reaction: The offender is responding to his or her situation in an immature, socially undesirable manner.
  "If the drunk driver isn't willing to pay the women's hospital costs and then get into an alcohol-abuse program, he deserves a jail sentence."

Repentance, Remorse: The actor expresses sorrow for what he or she did and vows to reform.
  "If the kid apologizes for hitting the policeman and really seems to feel sorry, then I say take it easy on him."

Impenitence: The actor expresses no sorrow or regret for the misdeed.
  "But if the kid acts tough and says he's glad he did it and he blames the police, then I say stick him in the slammer."

Reformation: The actor has reformed since committing the original act. In effect, the actor has neither repeated that offense nor committed others.
  "The Nazi colonel has never been in trouble since the war."

Recidivism: The actor has continued to violate rules or customs.
  "The army major kept doing awful things in South America. By selling drugs he's killing more people than he did in the war."

  (Note: *Repentance* in the present study means a verbal expression of regret and a commitment to improved behavior in the future. *Reformation* is a step beyond repentance in that reformation is displayed in actual changed behavior, not simply in a vow to change.)

Responsibility: The wrongdoer accepted blame for the offense he or she committed and did not try to escape or place the blame on others.
  "If the woman offers to pay for the injured boy's medical bills, then they should go easy on her."

Irresponsibility: The wrongdoer tried to escape responsibility for committing the offense.
  "Escaping to South America after the war and engaging in the drug trade rather than trying to compensate the Yugoslavs means the major deserves very strict punishment."

Elapsed Time Consequential: If the misdeed was committed a long time ago, punishment should be reduced.
  "The incident is long past. Let bygones be bygones."
  "The best way to get on with life is to try to forget what happened."

Elapsed Time Inconsequential: How long ago the misdeed was committed should not influence the consequences imposed.
  "He gave up his right to live by killing others, even though he did it 37 years ago."

State of Health Consequential: The transgressor's physical and mental health since the misdeed should be

State of Health Inconsequential: The transgressor's physical and mental condition since the misdeed should not

considered in determining consequences.
"They should go easy on him because of his sickness."

influence the consequences imposed.
"Even though he's sick, he still must pay for his crimes."

Age of Wrongdoer Consequential:
The age the transgressor has reached since the time of the misconduct should be considered in determining the consequences that are imposed.
"At his advanced age, he's not likely to be doing more crimes."
"The teen-age girl is young enough to learn to change her ways."

Age of Wrongdoer Inconsequential:
The age the transgressor has reached since the time of the misconduct should have no bearing on the sanctions imposed.
"Just because he's old doesn't mean he shouldn't be held accountable for what he did."

Obligations Consequential: Sanctions should be adjusted to responsibilities born by the transgressor.
"I would go easy on her because her family probably needs her financial contribution."

Obligations Inconsequential: Responsibilities that the transgressor might carry should not influence the kinds of sanctions imposed.
"If they put the drunk driver in jail, then he won't be able to make a living. Well, that's his tough luck. It'll maybe teach him a lesson."

Undue Burden: The proposed consequence would be an unreasonable burden for the offender to bear.
"If he's put in jail, he can't work and pay his debts, and that's not fair."

Reasonable Burden: The proposed consequence would apparently not pose an unreasonable burden for the offender
"Having her pay for the injured boy's medical bills isn't too much to ask."

Illegal Apprehension: The offender was taken into custody by illegal means, so aversive sanctions should be reduced or eliminated.
"Since the colonel was illegally abducted, he should go free."

Legal Apprehension: The offender was apprehended and treated lawfully, so there is no reason to alter sanctions for the way the offender has been treated.
"There's a law against stealing car radios, and they caught him red-handed, so he should get what's coming to him."

Indeterminate Response: The person's reaction after the offense tells nothing about whether he or she should be held liable for the misdeed.
"That he reformed after he went to South America shouldn't have anything to do with deciding on sanctions."

Guilty Response: The individual's reaction following the offense attests to his or her guilt.
"If he wasn't guilty, he wouldn't have run off to South America."

Fair Chance   A decision to be lenient in applying sanctions may be affected by a proposer's convictions about how to be fair to transgressors.

Second Chance: Everyone should be allowed an occasional mistake, so

Sanction Consistency: Any time a person commits an offense, he or she

an offender should not suffer severe consequences for the first misdeed.

> "If this was the woman's first accident, then they shouldn't put her in jail."

—without exception—should experience consequences deemed appropriate to that type of offense.

> "Unless sanctions are applied without exception, people won't learn to obey the law. Even if this is the first time the kid's been arrested, send him to juvenile hall."

Reparation Opportunity: Less severe punishment will enable the actor to provide reparations to the victims of his or her misconduct.

> "Jail-time would keep him from being able to pay for the medical bills of the injured parties and thus would cause them more suffering."

Absence of Reparation Opportunity: There is no reason to expect that the actor would provide more reparations to the victims of his or her misconduct if the actor were given less severe punishment.

> "The guy's insurance will pay the women's doctor bills, so it's okay to put him in jail."

Self-Improvement Opportunity: The consequence should be adjusted to permit the transgressor to engage in constructive self-improvement.

> "The girl should be in detention only during the summer vacation, so that she will not miss any days at school."

Self-Improvement Opportunity Unwarranted: There is no reason to think the transgressor would engage in self-improvement if the sanctions were less severe.

> "If the boy just goes to regular school and isn't put in detention, I don't think he's going to learn how to behave. He needs some strong discipline."
> "Trying to rehabilitate the major is a lost cause. He should be executed."

Vulnerable Life Stage: The transgressor is too young or too old to bear strict punishment.

> "I don't believe anyone should spend their last years in an awful place like prison."

Mature, Active Life Stage: The transgressor is a youth or adult of mature, active age.

> "He's old enough to know better and to pay the price for what he did."

<u>Extent of Damage</u> The degree of actual or potential harm is often a factor underlying judgments about the consequences wrongdoers should experience.

Minor Harm: The harm to others' welfare was slight.

> "At least the women weren't killed."

Major Harm: The harm to others' welfare was great.

> "Killing 109 is a heinous crime."

No Mention of Potential Harm: There is no suggestion that the offensive act might have caused even more damage than it did.

> "They killed 109. It couldn't have been much worse."

Greater Potential Harm: The offensive act carried the potential for causing even greater harm than it did.

> "She's lucky she didn't kill the boy."
> "What if the teacher had died from the stab wound?"

Low Degree of Future Threat: The likelihood that the offender would pose a threat to others' welfare in the future is slight.

"The woman probably learned her lesson by the accident. I doubt that she would drive again when she was taking medicine."

High Degree of Future Threat: The probability that the offender would be a future threat to others is great.

"Letting the boy loose on society would just encourage him to go on breaking the law, maybe even commit worse crimes."

Nondamaging Model: The undesirable example set by the actor's behavior would not likely be copied by others.

"People who saw the accident aren't apt to drive when they take medicine."

Damaging Model: The undesirable example set by the actor's behavior would likely be copied by others.

"She's a bad example for her sisters, so they shouldn't let her off easy."

Legal Status of the Behavior The question of whether there is a law governing an act may influence the type of consequence recommended for a wrongdoer.

Legal Act: There is no formal law to prohibit such an act.

"She wasn't actually breaking the law by driving under medication."

Illegal Act: There is a formal law governing the offense.

"He broke the law. So, as the saying goes, 'Commit the crime, you do the time.'"

Value Compatibility The decision about whether a given consequence is judged suitable can be affected by how well the consequence conforms to the proposer's moral principles.

Unduly Severe Consequence: A potential sanction conflicts with a moral conviction by imposing an undue burden on the offender.

"I am philosophically opposed to killing anyone; so no matter how bad the Nazi major acted, I could not agree with putting him to death."

Unduly Lenient Consequence: A potential consequence conflicts with a moral conviction in that the sanction fails to apply sufficiently strict punishment on the offender.

"I believe people should pay for their crimes to the same extent that their crimes caused pain and suffering for others; so I can't see letting the drunk driver off with a light sentence. He should at least go to F, pay medical bills for the two women, and lose his driver's license."

CONCLUSION

In this chapter we have contended that moral principles and the conditions under which the principles are applied are typically reflected in the rationales people offer to support consequences they recommend for wrongdoers. If principles are not included among the reasons respondents offer when they are first asked, "Why is that a suitable consequence?" then further inquiry may elicit the principles and conditions the person had in mind. There are several ways that such a follow-up inquiry can be phrased:

What rule of living did that person break?   And how serious do you think it was to break the rule?

Why did you suggest that particular consequence rather than some other one?

Were there any other possible consequences you considered when you chose this one? If so, why did you select this one over the others?

4

Purposes and Causes

In the context of the present study, the word *purpose* means the conviction a person holds about the function that a consequence is intended to perform. The word *cause* is being used in two ways—first, to mean the factors a person believes have produced an instance of wrongdoing and, second, to mean why the person believes a recommended consequence will accomplish its aim.

Whereas purposes and causes can both be reflected in the rationales people offer in support of proposed consequences, respondents in our opinionnaire survey offered purposes far more often than causes. Because the interview portion of our study asked specifically about purposes and causes, the interviews all yielded respondents' opinions about both factors.

THE PURPOSE OF A CONSEQUENCE

Statements of purpose identify the outcomes that consequences are supposed to produce. Those outcomes, in turn, are intended to achieve one or more of three ends:

1. To promote a moral principle and thereby contribute to the morally proper life. Example: Provide counseling for offenders so they will be equipped to fulfill their needs by morally acceptable means.
2. To furnish emotional satisfaction to persons who feel victimized—either directly or vicariously—by the wrongdoing. Example: Torture offenders in order to avenge a wrong.
3. To assuage the proposer's feelings of guilt and to express empathy for the offender. Example: Furnish shelter, food, and clothing for offenders whose misdeeds are thought to derive from their disadvantaged position in the social system.

As the following pages show, our analysis of respondents' rationales led us to devise a three-level scheme for reporting the purposes that respondents hoped consequences would accomplish. The first level is composed of ultimate outcomes that a sanction is expected to achieve. On the second level are aims thought to be instrumental in fostering ultimate outcomes. Third-level purposes also have an implementing function, serving to support purposes on the second and first levels.

People's reasons for the consequences they propose can include one or more of these levels. An illustration of such a three-level pattern of logic is seen in the reply of a California superior-court judge who was asked why he selected the particular sentences he assigned to lawbreakers.

> Society expects two things from me. It wants to be protected from criminals [Level I], and it wants me to produce crime-free individuals [Level II]. If I can introduce some accountability into the individual [Level III], then maybe we can get accountability into the system as well (Ryan, 1991, p. 9).

Although our six opinionnaire cases have all pictured individuals as the wrongdoers, it should be clear that transgression is often a group activity. The group may be a street gang, a business organization, a government agency, or an entire nation. Therefore, the purpose of a consequence can be to influence a group rather than simply an individual.

Our three-level scheme is not without its problems. First, a person who suggests a consequence may hope it will serve more than one purpose. Therefore, a given sanction may be intended to achieve aims at more than one level or to promote several outcomes at the same level. Second, the distinction among ultimate, instrumental, and implementing aims is not absolute. It is not always clear that a person who recommends a long prison sentence simply wants to harm the offender as an ultimate goal (Level I) or, as another possibility, that the proposer considers the pain of the prison term to serve only as an implementing device (Level III) for reforming the wrongdoer (Level II) and thereby maintaining a stable social system (Level I).

While recognizing the shortcomings of the three-level system, we believe it still has some utility as a method of categorizing apparent purposes people have in mind when they recommend consequences.

Level I: Ultimate Outcomes

Ultimate outcomes are end results that consequences are intended to produce. Fifteen ultimate-outcome purposes we identified are:

1. *Maintaining the Social System.* The goal in this instance is to support the existing social structure, uphold custom, and protect the orderly conduct of the society.
    "You can't run a society with people stealing other people's property."
    "The law is what holds the fabric of society together."
    "He's a constant menace to society."
2. *Teaching Right from Wrong.* The aim is to help wrongdoers distinguish between moral and immoral behavior and to encourage them to act in keeping with this distinction. (What constitutes *right* and *wrong* is determined by a respondent's values, which are not necessarily in concert with either formal laws or other people's moral values.)
    "A counselor in juvenile hall may be able to teach the girl why what she did was wrong."

3. *Teaching Respect for Authority.* The intent is to help offenders learn to obey the orders of people superior to themselves in a hierarchy of decision-making power and control. Such a sanction is founded on the conviction that people who bear the ultimate responsibility for the outcome of events must have the authority to direct the actions of others whose behavior affects those events.

   "If the boy gets some strict discipline, he may learn to respect the people in charge."

4. *Teaching Respect for the Law.* The purpose is to help offenders learn to abide by formal laws and regulations. This is a subtype under *Teaching Respect for Authority.*

   "Putting the drunk driver in jail, making him pay the women's medical expenses, and taking away his license should be enough to teach him to obey the law in the future."

5. *Teaching Accountability.* The intention is to hold people accountable for their actions in the hope that this will teach them to behave more responsibly in the future.

   "He has to learn that a price must be paid for what he did."

6. *Implementing the Law.* The aim is to ensure that the society is conducted in a consistent, predictable manner by applying the principle "Crime should not go unpunished."

   "She broke the law, so she faces the consequences."

7. *Acknowledging the Damage.* Harm done in wrongdoing should not go unrecognized. The imposition of sanctions draws the transgression to people's attention.

   "The victims' suffering should be acknowledged by punishing the German officers."

8. *Matching the Act.* The purpose here is to retaliate for wrongdoing with an act identical to the original offense, in other words, to repay in kind. Perhaps the best known version of this approach is the Judeo-Christian biblical injunction (*Holy Bible,* 1611, Exodus, chap. 21):

   > And if any mischief follow, then thou shalt give life for life, eye for eye, tooth for tooth, hand for hand, foot for foot, burning for burning, wound for wound, stripe for stripe.

   Gilbert and Sullivan's operetta *The Mikado* reflected this same purpose in one of Ko-Ko's songs: "My object all sublime I shall achieve in time—to let the punishment fit the crime."

   In our opinionnaire survey, this purpose was expressed through such comments as:

   "By killing others, he gave up the right to live."

   "Without consequences matching the offense, it will be repeated."

9. *Matching the Severity.* In this case the intention is not to respond to an offense with the same act as the original offense. Rather, the purpose is to answer with a different act that produces for the transgressor the same degree of pain, distress, loss, and inconvenience suffered by the victim of the misdeed.

   "The boy deserves to suffer as much as the cop he injured. Lock the boy up for a long time."

10. *Providing Specific Compensation.* The belief underlying this purpose is that the victims of misdeeds should be recompensed for harm they suffered.
> "If the woman who injured the boy is obligated to look after the boy's welfare,
>   it enables her to make amends for her actions."
> "The drunk driver must be held responsible for his actions by paying the
>   women's medical costs."

11. *Providing General Compensation.* Society in general deserves to be reimbursed for the harm wrought by the misbehavior.
> "If he's required to do some kind of community service, such as helping the
>   handicapped, it will help make up for what he did."

12. *Wreaking Revenge.* Vengeance is the ultimate outcome sought whenever someone who feels wronged cannot rest easy until sufficient punishment has been suffered by the offender.
> "The living relatives of the murdered Yugoslav partisans can feel that the
>   dead are somewhat avenged if the Nazi colonel is tortured to death."

13. *Reducing the Victim's Anger.* The consequence is intended to assuage the anger and sense of being abused that is felt by the recipient of the misdeed.
> "Knowing that the drunk driver has been put in jail should help relieve the
>   injured ladies' feelings of distress and injustice."

14. *Protecting Individuals' Rights.* Whereas the aim of maintaining the social system centers attention on society in general, the goal of protecting individuals' rights focuses on ensuring each person's freedom to enjoy the rights and privileges to which he or she is entitled. Two aspects of this purpose come into conflict whenever the rights of people other than the wrongdoer clash with the rights of the wrongdoer.
> "The girl who was selling drugs deserves the chance to change her life around;
>   so instead of sending her to jail, they should put her in a good foster home
>   where she can get proper guidance."

15. *Saving Money.* The recommended consequence is less expensive than others would be.
> "Killing him rather than putting him in prison saves taxpayers' money."

It should be apparent that a particular consequence can be intended to achieve more than one ultimate outcome. For instance, executing the German army major who supervised the killing of Yugoslavs would not only prevent him from disturbing the social system in the future by peddling illicit drugs, but it would also match the damage done to the Yugoslavs who had died and it would enable the remaining partisans to avenge the deed.

In effect, attempts to understand the mode of reasoning underlying people's assignment of consequences can usefully include discovering which ultimate outcomes their proposal is supposed to produce.

Level II: Instrumental Goals

The term *Instrumental Goals* identifies objectives that serve as tools for achieving the ultimate outcomes. We assigned four purposes to this set.

16. *Preventing Future Offenses.* The intention here is to preclude the wrongdoer from committing the same or similar offenses again.

"Because he seems mentally ill and cannot control his actions, he should be
put to death."

"Putting the girl in the detention center keeps her from selling dope."

17. *Effecting a Reformation.* In contrast to the first instrumental method, which
is simply intended to prevent a reoccurrence of past actions, this second one
has a more positive purpose, that of substituting constructive behavior for
the wrongdoer's past offenses. The aim is to equip people to fulfill their
needs by morally acceptable techniques.

"Sending the boy to a facility where he can get some counseling and proper
care could help him turn his life around."

18. *Deterring Others.* Frequently the purpose of consequences is not only to
alter the future actions of an offender but also to serve as an example to
others. Observers of the consequences are expected to recognize that if they
themselves engage in such wrongdoing, they, too, will experience like
sanctions.

"Seeing the kid put in jail ought to be a good lesson to the guys who hang
around with him."

"Making him tour schools and juvenile halls and tell how he got into trouble
might convince others not to commit crimes."

19. *Monitoring Offenders' Behavior.* The consequence permits responsible
parties to keep track of how responsibly the transgressor is conducting his or
her life.

"Putting her on probation means that there will be somebody regularly checking
up on the way she's getting along."

Level III: Implementing Aims

Pursuing Level-III aims should promote the attainment of one or more of the
second-level purposes and, as a result, should further the achievement of certain
first-level outcomes. We located seven purposes in this category.

20. *Removing an Offender's Opportunities.* The objective of this approach is to
obviate additional wrongdoing by changing the offender's environment in
ways that eliminate future chances to commit the same misdeed. This can be
accomplished either by moving the wrongdoer to a different setting and out of
temptation's way or by altering conditions of the original setting in which
the misdeed occurred.

Examples of moving offenders to different environments include sending a
thief to prison, placing a drug user in a rehabilitation center, or seating two
fighting pupils in opposite corners of the classroom.

Altering an original environment can involve such a change as:

"An alarm system on the car would start a siren howling, and that should scare
away any kid who wanted to steal the radio."

21. *Removing the Offender from the Influence of Unconstructive People.* This
technique is designed to free the offender from individuals who contributed to
wrongdoing in the past.

"Place the boy in a foster home, because his parents didn't care enough to get
him any help when they couldn't control him. They just kicked him out,
showing no love or responsibility."

22. *Providing the Offender Self-Improvement Opportunities.* This consequence represents a positive step beyond simply removing wrongdoers from an undesirable environment. The intention is to offer wrongdoers a chance to better themselves by being required to live in a constructive environment and engage in constructive activities.

> "If a really constructive program is offered in the detention facility, with job training, then that's where the girl should go, so she has a chance to learn legitimate ways to make money and solve her problems."

23. *Altering an Offender's Abilities, Values, and Attitudes.* Frequently the consequence is designed to change the wrongdoer rather than change the environment. It focuses on modifying the offender's ability and desire to misbehave. Such a goal may be accomplished either by reducing people's abilities or by enhancing their knowledge, skills, and attitudes. This option represents a step beyond simply opening opportunities in that it involves taking positive action to help ensure that offenders profit from the opportunity.

As an instance of reducing an offender's abilities, a judge in a court case ordered the implantation of a contraceptive device in a woman convicted of abusing infants she had born over the past few years. The judge's stated purpose was to eliminate the woman's chances of bearing more infants that she could mistreat (Ryan, 1991).

Enhancing people's abilities can include requiring that they acquire information and skill training, strengthening their sense of responsibility and accountability, and altering those values and motives that are believed to underlie future actions. Such specific improvements are intended to produce the reformation of behavior sought at Level II.

> "The drunk driver should be required to go to traffic school and maybe even join Alcoholics Anonymous so he'll pay better attention to how he behaves, especially when he's behind the wheel of an auto."

24. *Generating Affect.* The emotions that consequences of wrongdoing are most often intended to produce are negative ones, such as guilt, shame, fear, and remorse. The belief is that if a punishment causes offenders to feel bad enough, they will less likely repeat the misdeed and, it is hoped, will try to reform. Thus, generating painful affect can represent an attempt to alter a transgressor's attitudes.

> "Put her in jail to give her a good scare so she won't try selling drugs again."
> "The drunk driver needs to feel so guilty that he won't do it again."

25. *Reducing Negative Emotion.* The consequence is aimed at diminishing the anger, fear, or guilt that motivated the wrongdoer to commit the deed.

> "If the boy has a chance to talk out his problems with a therapist, he might not feel so disturbed about his life and so be ready to learn something better to do with his life."

26. *Harming the Offender.* A frequent objective of consequences is to inflict physical, psychological, or social harm on the wrongdoer. Physical damage involves corporal or capital punishment. Psychological injury can include threats, intimidation, fault finding, shaming, and harming people or objects that are treasured by the wrongdoer. Social damage can result from blemish-

ing an offender's reputation, isolating the offender, or boycotting services and products offered by the individual or group.

"The major deserves to suffer. Making him spend the rest of his life at hard labor in a prison would do it."

In conclusion, we are suggesting that the foregoing three-level framework is useful for categorizing the purposes reflected in the rationales people offer to support the consequences they advocate.

A CONCEPTION OF CAUSALITY

The term *conception of causality* is used here to mean a respondent's belief about the cause of the wrongdoing and/or why the recommended consequence would likely accomplish its purpose. This section opens with a description of four ways to view causality, then closes with a discussion of how people's recommended consequences can relate to their views of causation.

Four Ways to Perceive Causation

Over the centuries philosophers and scientists have conceived a wide variety of methods for classifying causes of behavior. Our intention here is not to catalogue all such methods. Rather, our purpose is to illustrate how four such approaches, which were implied in some of the respondents' comments about the six cases of wrongdoing, could serve as elements of the taxonomy. The four are labeled: (a) proximate and underlying causes, (b) heredity and environment, (c) a causal process, and (d) people's motives.

Proximate and Underlying Causes

One way to think about cause is in terms of a chronology of events. Things that happened earlier were the causes of events that later occurred. For example, a line of argument based on such a chronological perspective might go like this:

The reason the woman got into an accident was that the medication she had taken altered both her depth perception and her reaction time so that she ran into the boy on the bicycle. The reason she failed to heed the doctor's warning about driving a car when under medication was that she thought she was alert and could manage the auto adequately. The reason she thought she was alert was that she never had taken such medicine before and was not convinced that it could make her drowsy. The reason she had never taken such medicine before was that she had never suffered that same illness on earlier occasions. The reason she had never suffered was that . . . and so on.

In such a manner, proposed reasons can recede into the past to form an unending chain of causes. Philosophers have referred to this chain as the *infinite regress*—the belief that behind every event is a cause, and that this cause itself is an event produced by earlier causes. In other words, each effect is a cause of a future effect. Various terms have been used to reflect this chronological view of causation. The most recent links in the chain have been called *proximate, immediate,* or *precipitating* causes. Ones in the past have been called *prior, distant, underlying,* or *background* causes.

This historical view can serve as one way to categorize people's explanations of wrongdoing. Their proposals of causation can be ordered in terms of whether the causes they cite are proximate or underlying.

It can be convincingly argued, however, that our example of the woman driver is unduly simplistic. The example cites only a single cause behind each event, whereas it seems more likely that a cluster of causal factors operated at each juncture in the chronology. For instance, her failing to heed the physician's warning could have resulted from the following combination of elements: Although she recalled the doctor's advice, she still felt alert, she desired to go shopping, she was unwilling to face the inconvenience of walking or taking a bus, and more. Our proposal, then, is that at any moment several causal factors converge to determine an event. This is the concept of *multiple causation.*

It should be apparent that multiple causation can be viewed as functioning along two dimensions, vertical and horizontal. The vertical dimension is the chronological perspective, with multiple causes produced by the infinite regress of many reasons into the past. The horizontal dimension focuses on the combination of causal factors operating at a given moment.

If we adopt such a notion of multiple causation, including the vertical and horizontal dimensions, we find that the analogy of a historical chain of cause-and-effect links is no longer suitable. The chain can better be replaced by a very complicated fishnet, expanding in complexity as it retrogresses back through time.

A further element often included in such a causality equation is the concept of *differential power*, the presumption that some of the causal factors operating to produce an event exert stronger influence than do others. In the case of the woman who failed to abide by her doctor's advice, we could guess that her desire to go shopping was a stronger motivator of her behavior than was the doctor's warning.

To summarize, we are suggesting that one way to interpret people's proposals about causes of wrongdoing is to view their attributions within a framework of multiple causation that functions along vertical and horizontal dimensions, with some causal factors exerting more influence than others on any instance of misbehavior. Furthermore, within this same framework, the consequences people propose for wrongdoers can be analyzed in regard to how those consequences might be expected to achieve (to cause) their intended purpose.

Heredity and Environment

Probably the most popular broad-view mode of accounting for wrongdoing is in terms of a person's heredity and environment. From this perspective, the task of explaining misdeeds consists of proposing how a person's genetic inheritance interacts with the individual's surroundings to produce morally undesirable outcomes. The terminology of heredity-environment issues has varied from time to time—nature versus nurture, nativism versus cultural relativism, genetics versus social controls, maturation versus learning, innate characteristics versus acquired characteristics. Nevertheless, the basic question has been the same: How do inborn factors compare with environmental factors to produce instances of wrongdoing?

In the past, philosophers and social scientists often viewed this nature-nurture issue as a question of *either/or*. *Either* a youth's heredity *or* his environment was blamed for his misconduct. Today, those who study human behavior rarely, if ever, adopt such a view. Instead, they recognize the necessary interaction of both factors and thus seek to learn the manner in which inborn capacities combine with environmental influences to cause human events. The conflict among experts in the field, then, is not whether people's nature *or* their nurture is responsible for their wrongdoing. Rather, the debate is over how much —and in what fashion—one's genetic inheritance contributes to a given event as compared with how much—and in what fashion—different elements of the environment affect that event.

Consequently, in the effort to understand how people perceive wrongdoing, we can usefully provide in our taxonomy a way to categorize individuals' views of nature-nurture interactions. But before suggesting a scheme for this purpose, we should note two additional factors that some people presume are significant influences on wrongdoing —*luck* and *supernatural intervention*.

Citing *luck, chance, fate*, or *the breaks* to account for misdeeds is chiefly an admission of puzzlement, a giving-up on the attempt to offer an explanation in terms of hereditary and environmental factors.

The phrase *supernatural intervention* identifies a source of cause that transcends the everyday world. In monotheistic religions (Judaism, Christianity, Islam) the central source of influence (which is usually considered to be beneficent) is typically identified as God, Jehovah, Allah, or The Supreme Being. There also may be a subsidiary source of malevolent influence called the Devil, Satan, or Beelzebub. In polytheistic traditions (Hinduism, Shinto) a particular god or supernatural force may be blamed for particular types of wrongdoing (Thomas, 1988a). Thus, misdeeds may be attributed to God's will or to a person's being possessed by evil spirits.

Returning now to the heredity-environment issue, we can profitably recognize a variety of postulated nature-nurture theories as they apply to wrongdoing, with every theory representing a particular version of transactions among inborn and external influences. In the following overview, each theory is identified by a title, by key concepts on which it is founded, and by the role that consequences are assumed to perform in preventing future wrongdoing. The theories are organized within three principal categories—innate, environmental, and combined. The ones identified as *innate* stress inherited characteristics as reasons for misbehavior. Those labeled *environmental* cite factors in a person's surroundings as the principal determinants of wrongdoing. Theories referred to as *combined* are ones that attribute misdeeds to a rather evenhanded distribution of influence between nature and nurture.

Our purpose here is to describe the theories in a way that would enable us to infer the theoretical perspective reflected in the rationales respondents offer to support the consequences they recommend for wrongdoing. Our aim is not to assess the validity of the theories.

Theories Emphasizing Innate Influences. The most popular beliefs about the predominant influence of genetic inheritance on misbehavior involve convictions about innate character traits. Other versions of inborn causes of wrongdoing focus on learning disabilities that derive from genetic sources. The following discussion first addresses innate character traits, then treats inherited learning disorders.

Innate Traits of Personality. The term *character traits* typically is used to identify permanent personality qualities that are assumed to be the chief underlying causes of people's behavior. In past centuries, these qualities were referred to as *faculties*, meaning powers, capacities, or functions of the mind. Each faculty could be viewed as forming a scale extending from a large quantity of the trait to very little. For example, the scale for the faculty of *truthfulness* could range from a very high degree of veracity down to thoroughgoing mendacity. The faculty of *reason* could extend from brilliant intelligence to stupidity. There were similar scales for such ostensible traits as reverence, humor, will-power, imagination, kindness, sincerity, loyalty, diligence, temper, memory, and more.

Although trait theory is no longer called faculty psychology, it is still very much alive today and is often used to account for unacceptable behavior. From a heredity-environment perspective, trait theories can be placed in three major classes—innate, acquired, and combined. The following paragraphs focus on the innate variety. Later in this section acquired and combined types are discussed.

People who subscribe to an innate version are convinced that individuals who frequently break rules do so because of their flawed genetic composition. The belief is that wrongdoers were born with an uncontrollable temper, with a lack of concern for others' rights, with strong aggressive tendencies, with an inclination to lie, or the like. In the scientific community, this viewpoint has been lent a measure of credence by studies in criminology and sociobiology (Gleuck & Gleuck, 1974; Shoemaker, 1990, pp. 14-46; Wilson, 1978).

There are both psychological and physiological models of innate-trait theory, with the physiological form composed of two subtypes.

Innate Traits—Psychological Form. Proponents of the psychological variety hold that some people's genetic inheritance predisposes them to break rules and violate social conventions. It is not possible to tell by people's physical appearance which of them carry such predispositions. Hence, the inborn traits must be discovered either from observing people's behavior in situations involving morality or from analyzing individuals' responses on psychological tests. In other words, we cannot judge a person's character from his or her physical characteristics. The following comment from an opinionnaire in the present study suggests that the respondent subscribed to an innate trait theory:

> "Alcoholism is a disease, so the drunk driver needs medical treatment and
> psychotherapy."

Innate Traits—Physiological (Somatotypes). In contrast to the purely psychological variety, the somatotype version proposes that innate traits can be inferred from an individual's body build, on the belief that certain body shapes are related to particular qualities of temperament (Sheldon, 1940, 1942, 1949). Sheldon drew on earlier work by Kretschmer (1921) to postulate correlations between people's body structure and their general personality as well as certain specific traits. Sheldon maintained that elements of three basic body types comprised each individual's body build. The basic types were (a) the endomorphic (round, plump, soft), (b) the ectomorphic (thin, frail), (c) and the *mesomorphic* (hard, muscular). According to Sheldon, each person's body structure is a combination of these three types. Anyone's body build could be described by a score for each basic type on a scale from 1 to 7. A heavily muscled athlete might be rated 2-2-6, thereby recognized as predominantly mesomorph but with a bit of endomorph and ectomorph as well. In Sheldon's view, each somatotype is associated with innate personality characteristics:

> Endomorphic is associated with a viscerotonic temperament, characterized by extroversion and love of comfort. Mesomorphy is related to assertive, aggressive behavior, a somatotonic temperament. Ectomorphs are described as sensitive, shy, and introverted, referred to as a cerebrotonic temperament (Shoemaker, 1990, p. 18).

Applications of somatotype measurements to the analysis of wrongdoing have provided evidence that persistent delinquency is more frequently associated with mesomorphic body builds than with either ectomorphic or endomorphic types (Cortès & Gatti, 1972; Gleuck & Gleuck, 1950, 1956). Strong advocates of innate-trait theory contend that, like basic body structure, factors of temperament that predispose people to wrongdoing are part of an individual's genetic composition. However, other theorists have concluded that there is no such thing as "the delinquent personality" among mesomorphs or any other body type. Instead, mesomorphs may be more delinquent than others because their physical traits "equip them well for a delinquent role under the pressure of unfavorable sociocultural conditions" (Gleuck & Gleuck, 1956, p. 270).

Among the 562 people who participated in our opinionnaire and interview study, we found no one accounting for misdeeds by citing somatotype theory.

Innate Traits—Physiological (Physiognomic Form). A second variety of the physiological perspective is *physiognomic theory*, which regards people's facial features or expressions as indicators of character traits. This is a viewpoint with a long history. Proponents of the physiognomic viewpoint have held that a low forehead, scowling visage, shifty eyes, swarthy complexion, and similar features are indicators of untrustworthy character. No one participating in our research mentioned physiognomic factors as related to wrongdoing.

Genetically Based Learning Disabilities. Mental retardation, at least in some of its forms, has been seen as having a genetic component. A particular combination of genes is held responsible for an individual's intellectual impairment. Such impairment can occur in various degrees, so that an affected person may be either quite seriously below his or her agemates in mental ability or only slightly below average. In either case, the disability can be viewed as a cause of wrongdoing, since it diminishes the affected persons' ability to learn from their experiences. The mentally retarded often have difficulty understanding rules, judging the wisdom of the advice they receive, and predicting what consequences are likely to result from particular actions. Their impaired judgment can result in their being duped into wrongdoing by unscrupulous acquaintances, by their failing to carry out responsibilities, and by their breaking rules. In such a fashion, heredity can be seen as a contributing cause of misconduct. However, in the present study, none of the respondents attributed the misdeeds in any of the six cases to genetically based mental deficiency.

Theories Emphasizing Environmental Influences. All inter-pretations of cause that emphasize environmental sources of misbehavior are founded on the conviction that wrongdoing is learned, not inherited. Two features of environmental interpretations that are useful for comparing different people's views of causality are (a) the social units they believe are most significant and (b) the process by which these units exert their influence. First we consider types of social units, then the processes of influence.

In the present context, the term *social unit* refers to the way people are grouped for influencing an individual's moral behavior. For convenience of analysis, we have identified four levels of such units: (1) society in general, (2) major groups, (3) primary-contact groups, and (4) significant individuals.

Society in General. To account for the source of wrongdoing, some of the participants in our study offered such explanations as "Society is responsible for the way he's turned out" or "She's a victim of the social system." What precisely was meant by society was usually not explained, but the implication was that *society* referred to a monolithic set of values and an established form of social power and control that most members of a social system accept and support. In other words, the general populace and their institutions are in agreement about maintaining the established social structure and its moral values. The institutions include government (legislatures, the police, the courts), business and commercial interests, schools, churches, the family, and mass-communication media. Within such a conceptual scheme, incidents of wrongdoing are typically seen as the result of conflict between society and the individual's perceptions and habits. When wrongdoing occurs, society is at fault for failing to provide the proper upbringing of the individual and for imposing standards of conduct that conflict with the individual's needs. Typical statements by respondents in the present investigation that blamed wrongdoers' misdeeds on society were:

"Society doesn't care enough about kids."
"It's not the kid's fault. It's the underlying social structure."
"It's the way the establishment operates."

Major Groups. On this second level of social units, general society is pictured as a collection of large divisions or groups, each with characteristics that make its members different from those of other groups. Conflict between the groups results in people of one group—which is usually a group wielding the greatest power and social control—identifying behavior of people in another group as wrongdoing. Four common varieties of major groups are social classes, religious denominations, ethnic/national divisions, and occupational categories. A major-group interpretation of wrongdoing can be reflected in such remarks as:

"She was living in poverty. It's the rich exploiting the poor."
"Being in the army makes people act that way."

The most popular formalized major-group interpretation of delinquent behavior derives from Karl Marx's conception of conflict between a society's social-class levels, essentially a conflict between the *haves* and the *have-nots* (Marx, 1959). Upper classes are pictured as resisting lower class intrusions on upper-class privilege and power. The upper-class techniques of resistance include establishing rules governing property rights and personal behavior. Then members of the lower classes who fail to abide by those rules are judged guilty of lawbreaking and incur consequences deemed appropriate by those in authority. From this theoretical viewpoint, wrongdoing results from (1) the establishment of rules that favor the upper classes and deny the lower-class members a fair opportunity to exert their rights and fulfill their needs and (2) members of the lower classes violating the rules, either as an attempt to exert their rights or as a means of venting their anger and frustration at being victimized by an unjust social system.

A second kind of major-group conflict divides people along religious lines. At the core of each religious denomination is a set of convictions that binds the membership together. Actions in violation of these convictions are condemned by the members. From the viewpoint of a particular religious body, wrongdoing can result from a person outside that religious group acting in accordance with values contrary to those held by the denomination but in keeping with values held within the outsider's own group. For example, abortion is condemned in Catholic doctrine but not in a Unitarian belief system. Wrongdoing can also take the form of a member of a denomination willfully disregarding the sect's values.

Third are divisions along ethnic or national designations. The terms *ethnic* and *national* are combined here because in daily parlance they so often imply overlapping, similar, or identical meanings. Words typically intended to designate such groups are Spanish, Basque, African-American, Asian, Chinese, Cantonese, Anglo, Welsh, Scandinavian, Danish, Native American, Hopi, and the like. The phrase *national character* has been applied to the notion that the majority—if not all—of the people within a given ethnic or national category share in common certain values, habits, and/or personality traits. Positive characteristics that ostensibly typify such a group are reflected in such adjectives as *hardworking, clean-cut, honest, fun-loving, romantic,* and the like. Negative traits can include *dishonest, violent, lazy, hot-tempered, irrational, disloyal, petulant, sly,* and *scheming.* Differences between groups in such assumed characteristics can then be interpreted as a source of wrongdoing. In other words, actions considered normal and acceptable within one group may be condemned as misbehavior according to the standards of another group.

Fourth, influences linked to a person's vocation can be blamed for encouraging immorality. Occupations sometimes accused of exerting "a bad influence" on moral conduct include bar tending; law practice; prizefighting; television evangelism; military service; financial management; or employment in a gambling casino, in a carnival, or at a horse-racing track.

Behavior labeled wrongdoing can also result when members of a group apply different values to relationships within their membership than they apply to relationships with outsiders. In social-class struggles, as represented in the Robin Hood legend, the *have-nots* may honor property rights within their own class, yet consider the property of the *haves* to be there for the taking. Among religious bodies, the sacred relics of a sect may be respected by its own members, whereas relics of other sects are considered either foolish or vile and thus can be desecrated with impunity. In time of war, rules governing killing are typically applied differently to one's compatriots than to the enemy. Consequently, an act that would be considered misbehavior if aimed at a member of one's own group is not viewed as a misdeed when directed at outsiders.

Primary-Contact Groups. In such major groups as social classes, religious denominations, and national designations, any individual member is personally acquainted with only a small number of the people within the macroculture. In contrast, a person in a primary-contact group, or microculture, interacts directly with everyone in the group. Examples of microcultures are families, classrooms, church groups, social clubs, athletic teams, and street gangs.

When people cite a primary group as the cause of a person's misdeeds, they are not blaming any particular individual in the group for influencing a given member's values and behavior. Rather, they are suggesting that the group as a unit is responsible for the member's wrongdoing.

"Once the people around him were killing Yugoslavs, it probably seemed to him to be the thing to do."

"If he spent much time in bars, he probably saw the rest of them drinking and then driving, so he did it, too."

Significant Individuals. As the smallest unit of social influence, one or two individuals can be cited as the source of a wrongdoer's misconduct. The type of person most commonly accused of this highly significant influence is a parent.

"Maybe her mother encouraged the girl's drug dealing."

As another possibility, the individual exerting the crucial influence can be a teacher, a peer, an athletic coach, an admired motion-picture personality, or the like.

It should be apparent that the four social units described above are not mutually exclusive. In accounting for wrongdoing, people can allude to more than one of the levels.

"She was from a ghetto neighborhood where drugs and stabbings are an everyday occurrence, she belonged to a street gang, and her mother abused her."

"Not only does the army teach killing, but his commanding officer was unusually vicious and encouraged torture and violence."

In summary, one way to view environmental influence is in terms of the kind of group or individual that ostensibly contributed to the offender's committing a misdeed. Furthermore, the person who proposes a consequence may identify a group, organization, or type of individual that would be expected to implement the consequence.

Theories Combining Aspects of Heredity and Environment. In the above section, for convenience of discussion we completely separated hereditary from environmental forces; but in daily experience, thoughtful people rarely believe these two sources are entirely independent. Instead, nearly everyone who seriously considers such matters will judge wrongdoing to be the result of the interaction between a person's nature and nurture. Therefore, what distinguishes one person's view of causality from another's is usually (1) the aspects of genetic and environmental factors they include in their notion of cause and (2) the power or degree of influence they believe such factors exert on behavior. This means that a detailed description of anyone's causal attributions will require an in-depth identification of the hereditary and environmental aspects as well as the relative importance of those aspects in a person's conception of cause. Thus, in our opinionnaire study, as we interpreted the causal factors cited by respondents, we assumed that the particular factors that they cited were not the only ones they would believe contributed to wrongdoing. We imagined, instead, that the cited factors were probably the ones the respondents regarded as the most powerful. The interviews that we later conducted with 20 individuals helped support this assumption, because the interviewees often volunteered a multiplicity of influences that they assumed were operating in the lives of the two German army officers, the delinquent teenagers, and the pair of errant motorists.

A Causal Process

Oftentimes, people who identify a social unit as a cause of misconduct will neglect to explain the process by which they think such an environmental factor produced the wrongdoing. Their account goes no further than:

"Her mother was probably not a good parent."
"The people he hangs out with may think that getting drunk is no big deal."
"His parents didn't know how to treat him properly."

However, in accounting for misdeeds, other respondents add comments that imply something more specific about the process that led to an individual's misbehavior.

"It's the only way she knew how to act, since everybody she'd been around acted that way, too."
"Stealing stuff in the past worked out good for him, so he kept on doing it."

Such remarks can be accommodated in our taxonomy if we adopt a third perspective toward causality, that of proposing elements of the process by which physiological or environmental conditions effect their influence. The process is composed of four aspects of typical social-learning theory: (1) the array of moral events an individual can experience, (2) the values reflected in people's responses to such events, (3) the models a person imitates, and (4) the person's history of past consequences (Bandura, 1969, 1977). The quotations we use to illustrate the four steps have been drawn both from respondents' comments in the present study and from our one-month monitoring of news media.

Event Array. Each person's life pattern involves a particular variety of moral events that the individual has an opportunity to experience. What these events will be is determined by certain characteristics of the environments in which the individual has grown up. These characteristics include the people who determine what events an individual will be able to witness, the geographical settings of the events, and the complexity (and therefore comprehensibility) of stimuli in such settings.

"How was she to know it was illegal, since she was from a different culture?"
"His parents never let him play with other kids, so he didn't know how to get along with them."
"I imagine there was so much going on during the divorce that the child was confused about what it all meant."

Values Reflected in People's Reactions. People in the individual's environ-ment who witness moral incidents will often express, in word or deed, their opinion about the moral rectitude of participants in the incidents. From such experiences, the individual learns which moral values different people hold. The experience of hearing others' moral judgments helps determine the values an individual will adopt.

"The Nazi major was just following the orders of a superior."

"Since human life begins with conception, no matter when or how that girl terminates her pregnancy, it's murder."

"I don't mind their being on drugs, as long as they don't steal from me in order to pay for it."

Types of Models. Each individual's environment offers a particular set of people whose traits and behavior the individual could choose to copy. Social-learning theories, in effect, are typically founded on the belief that much of human behavior is acquired through an individual observing others' actions, then selecting certain of these actions to incorporate into his or her own behavior repertoire (Bandura, 1977). The people chosen as models are ones the individual views as being successful. In other words, admired models are ones whose appearance and actions yield rewards that the observer would also like to receive.

"He probably started stealing because he'd seen guys in his neighborhood steal in order to get things they couldn't afford to buy."

"She wanted to be accepted as a hot shot member of a tough gang, and to do that she thought she had to sell drugs so they'd think she was great."

"If the woman receives severe punishment, it may be a lesson to others."

The Effect of Past Consequences on Future Behavior. Everyone has a history of consequences that were experienced in past moral situations, and that history influences how the person will act in the future. This conviction rests on the presumption that the more a new situation is interpreted to be like past situations, the more readily the individual will adopt the same actions that resulted in acceptable consequences in the past.

"The Nazi major was willing to carry out the killings because he'd seen what had happened to others when they hadn't followed their superiors' orders."

"The man was used to stopping at a bar for a drink or two after work, and he'd always been able to drive home without getting into a wreck."

The belief that the consequences recommended for current misdeeds could influence future behavior was reflected in many of the rationales respondents offered in the present study.

In summary, we are suggesting that when we find process statements in the rationales respondents offer, we improve our understanding of their modes of moral reasoning.

People's Motives

In the interview phase of our study, one of the questions we asked was: "What do you think caused the person to do wrong?" In response, a large proportion of those interviewed cited the offender's apparent motives more often than they cited genetic or environmental factors. Thus, the cause of wrongdoing can be cast in terms of the motives that apparently stimulate people to commit offenses. The following list was generated from both the interview and questionnaire responses we collected.

Acquisitiveness. To obtain possessions.
  "He wanted things that he couldn't afford, so he stole them."
Attention Getting. To gain attention from others.
  "Maybe she didn't get much attention at home, and earning money from selling drugs would get her attention and make her feel better."
Curiosity. To discover the nature of a new experience.
  "Perhaps the girl was just inquisitive. She wanted to know what it was like to sell drugs, so she tried it out."
Harmavoidance/Blameavoidance. To defend oneself from physical or psychological damage.
  "When she stabbed the teacher, she thought he might die and then nobody would be able to identify her, so she'd get away with it."
  "The kid hit the policeman out of fear, a kind of knee-jerk reaction to protect himself when he was suddenly caught."
Loyalty. To remain faithful to one's obligations.
  "The major felt bound to carry out the orders of his superior officer."
Revenge—Indiscriminate. Strike back at the world in general in order to avenge assumed ill treatment at the hands of society.
  "Maybe the boy was so upset about his life that he wanted to hurt anyone or anything that got in his way."
Revenge—Targeted. Harm particular individuals in order to avenge assumed ill treatment at the hands of those individuals.
  "He could have been trying to make his parents feel bad for putting him out of the house."
Self Determination. To guide one's own life without others interfering.
  "The woman intended to go shopping, no matter what the doctor told her."
Social Approval. To win the acceptance of a particular person or group.
  "She probably started selling drugs because her friends thought it was real cool, and she didn't want to put them down."

Notions of Causality Embedded in Rationales

Finally, a question can be asked about how people's ideas of cause can influence their proposals of consequences. There are at least two ways:

First, a recommended consequence can be intended to correct a supposed cause of misdeeds. This linking of a consequence to an assumed cause may be reflected in such comments as:

  "Making him go to Alcoholics Anonymous could maybe stop him drinking so he won't get into any more accidents by being drunk."
  "The boy's parents didn't know how to raise him right, so he should be sent to a detention home where the counselors would treat him better."

Second, people's ideas of causation can explain why they think the consequences they recommend will have a desirable effect.

  "If she's locked up for a while, she may get the message that stabbing people is a bad idea."
  "They could get the boy into a good boys' club where he'll be with guys who set a good example."
  "The drunk driver should be required to undergo alcohol-abuse therapy and education."

Throughout the present study, the notion of cause was found in a variety of respondents' rationales, yet the word *cause* itself was rarely used. Instead, causation typically appeared only by implication. Consider, for example, the case of the girl who stabbed a teacher at the time the girl was apprehended in a drug sale. The belief that poverty and inadequate child-rearing practices were causes behind such wrongdoing can be inferred from a respondent's suggestion that "the girl's mother should be helped financially and should be educated to care properly for her child." In the case of the boy who hit the police officer, the idea that the disordered relationship within the family was a cause of the misdeed is implied in the recommendation that "the boy and his parents need intensive counseling."

CONCLUSION

In this chapter we have suggested how various purposes of consequences as well as ideas of causation may be reflected in the reasons people give to explain the sanctions they recommend for wrongdoing.

5

Feasibility and Agents

The two final divisions of our taxonomy focus on how practicable a consequence may be and on who has the right to suggest or impose consequences. In our opinionnaire survey, these two matters were rarely mentioned by respondents. However, in the interviews we conducted, when we questioned people about such things, the interviewees clearly had opinions ready to express. Thus, we concluded that the failure of questionnaire respondents to include in their rationales any mention of practicability and of the right to impose sanctions was not because they lacked convictions about these matters. Rather, it apparently was because they considered moral principles, purposes of consequences, and issues of cause more important for defending the consequences they suggested.

CONSEQUENCE FEASIBILITY

The phrase *consequence feasibility* refers to how practicable it would be to implement a consequence. Sometimes a sanction that would seem quite effective in achieving a given purpose is rejected because it could not reasonably be implemented. Hence, the person selects an alternative consequence as the one to apply. Thus, the process of choosing a sanction includes answering the question: How likely can a particular consequence be carried out in view of feasibility considerations?

In the taxonomy, we provide for identifying seven feasibility considerations. They relate to unacceptable side effects, inconvenience, funds, facilities, personnel, and effectiveness of goal achievement.

Unacceptable Side Effects. There are numerous kinds of unwanted side effects. Some involve excessive harm to the wrongdoer. For example, corporal punishment may cause permanent physical injury. Caustic public ridicule may lead to extreme social ostracism. Imprisonment can place the wrongdoer under the long-term, intimate influence of hardened criminals.

"Confiscating his driver's license may cost him his job."
"Incarceration would do nothing but exacerbate the boy's antisocial attitude."

"If she's taken from her home, she can't help her mother and sisters."

Undesired side effects may also result for people other than the wrongdoer. For instance, jailing a parent may leave the family without a source of financial support. Executing a felon may motivate the felon's relatives to seek revenge on the judge or jury that tried the case. Furthermore, the negative reaction of the general public to putting a convicted rapist on probation may render that consequence impractical.

"Letting him go free just increases the possibility that he'll drive drunk again."

Inconvenience:. Potential sanctions are sometimes rejected because they appear unduly troublesome.

> "The parents should both come for therapy along with the kid, but I doubt they would want the bother."

> "If the teacher kept the girl in after school for a week, that would mean the teacher couldn't tend to her own business, like buying groceries or going to the bank."

Funds. The monetary cost of applying the sanction can also be a consideration in selecting a consequence.

> "She needs lengthy counseling by an expert, but who would pay for it?"

> "Having the taxpayers spend money to keep him in prison for years isn't worth it, so they might as well hang him."

Facilities. A further aspect of feasibility involves the place and equipment needed to impose a consequence.

> "A good foster home would be best for her, but there may not be a good one available."

> "The jails are already overcrowded, so it's better to find something else to do with him."

Personnel. Implementing a sanction may also require particular types and numbers of people that are not readily available.

> "There aren't enough probation officers to give proper guidance to all the cases they're assigned, so putting the boy on probation isn't suitable."

Effectiveness of Goal Achievement. A sanction may be rejected because it would not likely accomplish the desired end.

> "The girl needs job training; locking her up would help no one."

> "Putting the woman in jail would prevent her from paying the victims' medical costs."

> "Clustering criminals together is cost-effective but sociologically unsound."

The foregoing list of feasibility factors should be regarded as illustrative rather than as definitive. For example, other considerations include time constraints, political pressures, and the age of the offender.

AGENT QUALIFICATIONS

This final category refers to people's beliefs about which individuals or agencies have the right and responsibility to assign consequences for wrongdoing. Nearly all of the respondents in our questionnaire survey were themselves willing to suggest sanctions for wrongdoers in the six illustrative cases. However, a few people elected not to propose consequences, asserting that the right to make such a decision lay elsewhere.

In the interview portion of this investigation, we divided the qualified-agent issue into two questions. First, we asked what sorts of people had a right to express an opinion about the kinds of consequences to impose. Next, we asked who had the right to see that sanctions were actually carried out. Whereas all 20 interviewees felt that everyone has a right to offer an opinion about consequences, they differed in their views of who had the right to see that the consequences were administered.

For purposes of the taxonomy, we identified six types of agents: a supreme being, the natural course of events, a government agency, a religious agency, peers, and family.

A Supreme Being. In Shakespeare's play about Danish kings, when Hamlet asked the ghost of his father what should be done about Hamlet's mother marrying the murderous uncle, the ghost advised Hamlet, "Leave her to heaven." Such was the opinion of respondents in the present study who contended that:

"No one has the right to put others to death. God is the one to decide when a
person should die."

The Natural Course of Events. Some people subscribe to the belief that justice is automatically provided by the nature of the universe. This is the concept of *immanent justice*, which Piaget (1966) found to be rather common among young children. It is a conviction that misdeeds will be punished during the natural order of events, so it is unnecessary for anyone to suggest sanctions for wrongdoing.

"Someplace along the way, he'll get what he deserves."

"It'll catch up with her some day."

A Government Agency. Official law-enforcement units are widely recognized as the bodies responsible for assigning consequences when formal laws are violated.

"It's up to the courts."

"A jury should decide."

"The police are responsible for saying what to do."

A Religious Agency. Representatives of a religious denomination can be viewed as the proper selectors of consequences.

"The church will determine if the soldiers should be excommunicated."

Peers. People who are considered to be of the same social status as the offender may be thought best suited to identify sanctions.

"The kids at school will make her suffer for what she's done."

Family. Parents are often regarded as the ones qualified to set sanctions for the misbehavior of their offspring.

"Her mother had better do something about that girl."

"It's his parents' right to punish him."

In addition to the above six agents, others sometimes cited in different cases than those used in the present study are athletic coaches, club leaders, business executives, labor union officials, and more.

CONCLUSION

When people are asked to tell why they have suggested a particular consequence in a case of wrongdoing, only a few spontaneously include considerations of feasibility in their proposal. This usually happens when an individual explains why one potential sanction was rejected in favor of another. But when people are specifically asked why they chose one consequence over another, as was done in the interview portion of our study, a far larger number mention factors of feasibility.

When faced with the task of proposing sanctions for wrongdoing, a few people decline on the grounds that they are not qualified to offer such a recommendation. However, most are still ready to suggest consequences they believe wrongdoers should face, even though they might not be willing to impose those consequences under real-life conditions. Such was true of participants in the present study.

Part III

Group and Individual Comparisons

As explained earlier, the study reported in this book was conducted in five stages.

Stage 1: The Opinion Survey. Printed opinionnaires describing six cases of wrongdoing were administered to six groups of people—a total of 542 respondents—who were asked (a) to recommend consequences for the wrongdoers to experience and (b) to tell why they thought their recommendations were appropriate.

Stage 2: The Derived Taxonomy. The completed opinionnaires were analyzed in order to extract information useful in creating a taxonomy of the moral reasoning behind the respondents' proposed consequences. At the same time, an informal survey of one month's issues of newspapers and television news programs was conducted so as to expand the taxonomy's components somewhat beyond the items extracted from the opinionnaires. The results of this stage formed the contents of Part II.

Stage 3: Group Comparisons. The taxonomy was used for categorizing the answers offered by each of the six groups that completed the opinionnaires. Comparisons of the groups' answers form the contents of the first four chapters of Part III. Chapter 6 describes the consequences suggested by the participants. Chapter 7 summarizes the moral principles and the conditions implied in the respondents' answers, whereas Chapter 8 focuses on the aims of consequences and on participants' opinions about causation, feasibility, and agents' qualifications. Chapter 9 compares the opinions of females and males.

Stage 4: Moral-Reasoning Styles. The major categories of the taxonomy served as the source of the questions that 20 participants were asked during interviews about the six cases of misdeeds described on the opinionnaires. Results of this investigation of overt cognitive style are described in Chapter 10.

Stage 5: Lessons Learned, Practical Implications, and Further Research. As the final step, Chapter 11, which constitutes Part IV, suggests (a) some lessons learned and some old lessons reinforced by the results of this research, (b) a variety of ways the results of this kind of study can be applied in everyday life, and (c) research projects that could promote further understanding of the moral-reasoning patterns that undergird people's proposals of what wrongdoers deserve.

In preparation for the contents of Part III, the remainder of this introduction addresses (1) characteristics of the project's principal data-gathering methods and (2) the ways opinionnaire and interview responses were scored.

FEATURES OF THE DATA-GATHERING METHODS

As already noted, the data on which the contents of this book have been based were collected by opinionnaires administered to 542 people and by interviews conducted with an additional 20 respondents. These two data-gathering methods were expected to make separate contributions to the study.

The opinionnaires sampled the ideas of a large number of people, thereby furnishing a diversity of viewpoints from which to construct a taxonomy of moral reasoning. And because opinionnaires were completed by substantial numbers of people from six different social settings, likenesses and differences among the six groups could be examined, and we could speculate about possible causes of such results. However, as a data-gathering technique, the opinionnaire survey proved to be weak in three respects. It failed to elicit information about every respondent's position in regard to all five categories of the taxonomy, it did not reveal the pattern of reasoning people used in arriving at their answers, and it did not permit respondents to ask questions that might clarify perplexing aspects of the cases of wrongdoing.

To compensate for the shortcomings of the opinionnaire approach, the 20 interviews were conducted after the opinionnaire study had been completed. Although the interviews elicited replies from a very limited number of people, they did provide information about each respondent's opinions regarding all five components of the taxonomy. The interviews also revealed individuals' style of overt reasoning and provided opportunities for clarifying aspects of the cases that the interviewees found confusing when they first read the cases.

SCORING PROCEDURES

The bulk of the information in Chapters 6, 7, 8, and 9 derives from the opinionnaire survey. However, comments from the interviews are also occasionally included to illustrate something about participants' patterns of thought as they arrived at their decisions.

Data from the 542 opinionnaires were compiled in the following manner. First, each item in the taxonomy was assigned a code number. The code numbers were listed on a series of scoring sheets, with each number followed by: (a) the description of the item as it appeared in Chapter 3, 4, or 5; (b) sample responses from the questionnaires to illustrate instances of such an item; and (c) an occasional explanatory comment to distinguish a particular item from others with which it might be confused. The coded sheets were used to guide the scoring of questionnaire answers.

Next, the two authors of this work—Thomas and Diver-Stamnes—separately used the scoring sheets for interpreting the answers on a sample of 20 randomly selected questionnaires (a total of 120 cases of wrongdoing) and for reporting the interpretations as code numbers on record forms. The two raters' results were then compared to determine how closely they agreed on the appropriate codes to assign each answer. As shown in column A of Table III-1, the two raters' first attempt resulted in considerable disagreement. It was apparent that portions of the scoring guide required greater precision so that different raters would arrive at the same judgments. When the scoring guide was revised, the interrater agreement reached the levels indicated in column B.

Because the agreement between raters was less than perfect, in the final scoring of opinionnaires the following procedure was adopted to reduce the influence of rater bias during group comparisons of opinionnaire answers. Within each of the six sampling groups, opinionnaires were divided into a female set and a male set. The members of each set were ordered randomly and assigned sequential identification numbers. In the process of tabulating the entire collection of 542 opinionnaires, Diver-Stamnes scored the odd-numbered ones and Thomas the even-numbered. Thus, any differences in scoring decisions that might still exist between the two raters would be balanced across the sets and groups.

All of the quantitative results reported in Part III are cast as percentages. Statements about differences between one group and another follow the popular convention in social-science research of identifying differences in terms of whether they extend beyond the .05, .01, or .001 levels of statistical significance. In other words, a difference between groups that would likely occur less than 5 times out of 100 simply because of measurement or sampling error is reported as significant at the .05 level. Likewise, differences large enough to occur by chance less than once in 100 or once in 1,000 are reported as significant at the .01 and .001 levels, respectively.

Table III-1

Interrater Reliability Levels
(in percentages)

Taxonomy Category	Column A	Column B
Type of Consequence	76	94
Moral Principles	73	96
Conditions in Applying Principles	48	70
Purposes of Consequences	58	84
Cause	51	79
Feasibility	100	100
Qualified Agents	100	100

6

Proposed Consequences

This chapter answers two sets of questions. Among the 542 individuals who completed opinionnaires:

1. What range of consequences to be faced by offenders were proposed in the six cases of wrongdoing, and which consequences were most often recommended? What typical rationales were offered in support of the consequences, as indicated by how people responded to the question of why they thought their proposed consequences were the most suitable?
2. What significant similarities and differences were found among the six groups that composed the entire sample of 542 respondents? What are likely reasons for the groups' likenesses and differences?

We may recall that the six cases represented three pairs of moral-decision situations. Within each pair, the offenders' misdeeds were very similar. Yet also within each pair the two cases differed from each other in several ways. For example, both Nazi officers had contributed to the deaths of Yugoslav partisans during wartime, but the two differed in their military rank, in the roles they played in the executions, and in their postwar behavior and state of health. The two drivers who caused auto accidents were alike in being under the influence of mind-altering substances, but they differed in gender and in their reasons for ingesting the substances. The teenage girl and boy were alike in age and in committing two misdeeds, but they differed in gender, in the exact form of their misdeeds, and in their family backgrounds. For each pair of cases, the consequence options offered on the opinionnaire were identical for the two Nazi officers, identical for the two motorists, and nearly the same for the two teenagers.

In the scheme described in Part II for classifying consequences, sanctions were located under six categories—physical treatment, property, rights and privileges, labor, verbal responses in private and public, and indeterminate reactions. Three forms of support activities were also identified—material, psychological, and instructional. References to that scheme appear in the following discussion.

THE DIVERSITY OF CONSEQUENCES AND
ONES MOST OFTEN RECOMMENDED

In all six cases of wrongdoing, the great majority of the 542 respondents selected one of the consequences listed below the particular case description, or else they combined elements from two or more of the listed options. Only a small proportion offered consequences of their own devising. For the two Nazi officers, 10% of respondents suggested their own alternatives. For the girl who sold drugs and the boy who stole the car stereo, nearly 15% created their own proposals. For the drunk driver, 18% offered such alternatives as requiring the offender to undergo treatment for alcohol abuse or to stand for jury trial. Slightly more than 11% created consequences for the woman driver who had injured a bicyclist.

In trying to explain this tendency of people to choose among the listed options rather than create their own, we speculated that such behavior might result from a combination of four factors. The first could be labeled *simplicity and ease*. For most people, if not all, it is easier to select from a list of choices than to generate other alternatives.

A second factor is the likelihood that the sorts of options listed under the cases were types of consequences commonly imposed in the respondents' societies for the kinds of misdeeds represented in the cases. Sentencing convicted criminals to death or to a long prison term is a sanction frequently applied to people who kill others. Placing juveniles in detention or under the supervision of a probation officer is a popular treatment for youthful offenders. Serving a jail term, paying a fine, assuming victims' medical costs, and losing an operator's license are consequences often applied to motorists who break the law. Hence, for most respondents, the listed options may have appeared both familiar and appropriate.

Third, perhaps many of the participants had not previously thought carefully about what kinds of consequences are most suitable, under what circumstances, and for what types of misbehavior. If they had not considered these issues on earlier occasions, they would not likely be prepared at this time to offer alternative consequences or to offer well-reasoned rationales in defense of their proposals.

A fourth factor is the possibility that participants were influenced in their approach to the opinionnaires by their previous experience with school assignments. Students' acquaintance with multiple-choice formats on tests and questionnaires may have caused them to approach the opinionnaire task with expectations brought from their earlier encounters. They were asked to "choose from the following actions the one you prefer in this case." In other words, the high incidence of respondents recommending the listed consequences rather than devising other options is likely a function—at least in part—of the multiple-choice form of the alternatives, even though provision was also made under each case for people to suggest other consequences.

Although only a small minority of participants contrived their own options, their creations were so diverse that the total number of alternative consequences for a given offense ranged from 17 for the girl selling drugs to 26 for the boy caught stealing a car radio. The assortment of consequences recommended for a given instance of wrongdoing is suggested by the following samples from two of the cases—the former Nazi major who trafficked in illegal drugs and the woman who drove her car while she was under medication:

> *For the major.* Death, lifelong imprisonment, be tortured, pay a large fine, be stripped of all his property, provide money for the victims' families, labor for the victims' families, study the misery suffered by the families, furnish community service, offer a public apology, receive public censure and humiliation, stand for jury trial, be set free to return to South America, or be freed of war crimes but prosecuted for recent drug dealing.
>
> *For the woman motorist.* Jail sentence (for a year, for a few months, for a few weeks), pay the victim's medical costs, pay a large fine, lose her driver's license (for a few months, for a year, for five years), provide community service, engage in work that directly benefits the victim, furnish transportation for the victim, attend driver-training classes, stand jury trial, be punished "as specified by the law," or be set free.

The frequency of different consequences as suggested by 2% or more of the 542 subjects is displayed in Table 6-1. Although many respondents recommended the death sentence for both of the former Nazi officers, 16% more would execute the major (57%) than would execute the colonel (41%).[*] Most respondents would jail the colonel for life (57%), whereas a notable minority would set him free to return to South America (18%). Of those who recommended greater leniency for the colonel than for the major, many supported their decision by citing differences in the two men's life-styles since World War II. The colonel had become a law-abiding citizen, whereas the major was involved in illicit drug trade. Furthermore, the colonel, unlike the major, was now in poor health. Among the respondents who would free the colonel (18%) or the major (4%) to return home, many did so because they believed the moral rules of peacetime did not apply during a war. In wartime, they said, killing the enemy was a soldier's duty and thus should not be considered the same as murder in peacetime.

In the cases of the two teenagers, far more people would recommend a year's detention for the girl (65%) than for the boy (35%). One reason for such a difference could be that the remaining alternative listed below each case was not exactly the same. According to that second option, both the girl and boy would be placed under the supervision of a probation officer and enrolled in school, but the girl would be able to return to her own family, while the boy would be placed in a foster home. However, the difference between returning home and being assigned to a foster family did not appear to be the principal reason that so many more would send the girl to a juvenile facility. In the rationales that respondents offered to support their decisions, a number of respondents identified the girl's drug peddling and stabbing as more serious crimes than the boy's thievery and his striking the police officer. In addition, more respondents expressed sympathy for the boy's homeless state than for the nature of the girl's home life.

---

[*] All percentage differences identified in this section are statistically significant well beyond the .001 level.

As for the two motorists who caused accidents, the majority of respondents would require that both of them pay the victims' medical expenses and a $1,000 fine. Only a minority would jail the motorists. Generally, the respondents denounced both drivers for their "stupidity" and "irresponsibility" in risking others' lives. However, the penalties for the drinking driver were greater than those for the woman who drove while under medication. Imprisonment was recommended for the man by 35% of the respondents, but for the woman by only 20%. The man would more often be assessed a large fine (61%) than would the woman (50%). He would also more frequently be expected to pay medical costs (63% compared with 56%). A main reason for the more severe treatment of the man appeared to be the highly emotional condemnation of drunk drivers that many of the participants expressed in support of their recommendations.

Comments that people offered in support of their suggestions often revealed that not everyone perceived the influence of a particular consequence in the same way. Consider, for instance, three conflicting expectations for what would result if the youth who stole the car radio was sent to a juvenile detention center:

Table 6-1

Frequently Recommended Consequences
(in percentages; N = 542)

			The Cases			
Recommended Consequences	*Army Colonel*	*Army Major*	*Girl & Drugs*	*Boy & Stereo*	*Drinking Driver*	*Medicated Driver*
Death	41	57				
Imprisonment:						
For Life	57	37				
For One Year			65	35	18	33
For Unspecified Time			2	6	2	2
Pay Large Fine					50	61
Pay Victim's Medical Expenses				2	56	63
Driver's License Revoked					21	19
Supervised Probation			13	55		
Counseling/Therapy			8	11	4	
Attend School			8	60		
Foster Home			3	61		
Set Free	18	4	3	3		

Note: In none of the cases do the cited percentages add up to 100%. This is because (a) some respondents cited more than one consequence and (b) those consequences proposed by less than 2% of the participants have been omitted from the table.

"He'd come out of juvenile hall worse than when he went in. The harsh treatment and restrictions there would simply antagonize him, and the other inmates would teach him to be more of a criminal than he already was."

"A period of detention could give him what he needs—some strict discipline."

"The boy should have help in developing a positive self image and a feeling of empowerment. A caring, supportive counselor at the detention facility could do that for him."

GROUP SIMILARITIES AND DIFFERENCES

As explained in Chapter 2, the 542 people who filled out opinionnaires represented six social settings identified as:

1. Polk-Metro Public High School in a high-crime district of a large West Coast city (132 students).
2. San Pablo Parochial High School in a small western city with a relatively low crime rate and a moderately high income level (166 students).
3. Makai Public High School in a Hawaiian seacoast town with a predominantly lower-income population (31 students).
4. Pele Community College, a two-year institution in the state of Hawaii's largest urban area, where the 24 respondents attended college on a part-time basis while working at full-time jobs during the day.
5. Northcoast University, located in a rural area of the northwestern United States, where the 63 participants in this study were graduate students enrolled in a teacher-education program.
6. A high school (44 respondents) and a university (82 respondents) in a major Saudi Arabian urban center.

The frequency with which each group recommended the most commonly mentioned consequences is shown in Tables 6-2, 6-3, and 6-4. It is apparent that comparing each respondent group with every other group so as to discover which differences between pairs are statistically significant is a very time-consuming task. To simplify that task for readers, we have identified which differences between pairs of groups exceed a .05 level of statistical significance and have displayed the results in Table 6-5. In effect, Table 6-5 contains only the differences from Tables 6-2, 6-3, and 6-4 significant beyond a .05 level.

Our analysis of the data in the four tables was guided by two sets of criteria, the first entitled *severity of consequences* and the second *initiative in proposing consequences.*

Severity of Consequences

The phrase *severity of consequences* identifies an imagined scale that extends from harsh, confining punishment at one end to gentle, liberating treatment at the other. In other words, such a scale focuses on the degree of physical or psychological pain a sanction would likely cause and on the extent to which the consequence restricts the offender's freedom for self-determination. On the opinionnaire, the consequence options listed under each case were intended to represent different points along such a scale. For example, in cases 1 and 2, death was considered the most severe, life imprisonment rather less oppressive,

Table 6-2

Group Comparisons — Cases 1 & 2
(in percentages)

	The Groups					
Proposed Consequences	*Polk-Metro High*	*San Pablo Parochial*	*Makai High*	*Pele C.C.*	*Northcoast Univers.*	*Saudi Arabia*
	N = 132	*166*	*31*	*24*	*63*	*126*
Case 1: Ordering Partisans' Executions						
Death	55	32	38	42	40	40
Prison	33	37	28	29	38	29
Set Free	13	25	28	42	6	12
Case 2. Supervising Partisans' Executions						
Death	54	44	63	33	37	72
Prison	43	43	28	25	46	16
Set Free	.3	4			4	
Freed on war activities but prosecuted for drug dealing	4				13	

Note: In Tables 6-2, 6-3, and 6-4, consequences in roman type identify options that had been listed under a case description on the opinionnaires. Consequences in *italic* type identify options introduced anew by respondents on their own initiative.

and "set free" the most charitable. While this ordering of the three options conforms to typical perceptions of severity in criminal law and among the majority of the general public, it was apparent in the present investigation that a few respondents considered life imprisonment more brutal than death. This minority viewpoint was reflected in such comments as "Death's too easy; put him in prison at hard labor" and "For what he did, he should be locked up to suffer lifelong guilt and regret instead of escaping his misery by just being put to death." However, for purposes of comparing our six respondent groups from the viewpoint of consequence severity, we adopted the perception of the majority. This meant that in the cases of the two army officers, death was considered the most severe, with the remaining consequences deemed less harsh. In Cases 3 and 4, sentencing the teenage girl and boy to a year in a detention center was judged to be more severe than placing them on probation and sending them to school. In cases 5 and 6, jailing the motorists for a year was considered harsher punishment than requiring them to pay a fine, to pay for the accident victims' medical treatment, or to lose their license to drive.

With consequence-severity as an appraisal criterion, we inspected Tables 6-2, 6-3, and 6-4 to answer three questions about the six groups of respondents:

1. In general, how harsh were the sanctions proposed by one group in comparison to the severity of sanctions proposed by the others?

Table 6-3

Group Comparisons — Cases 3 & 4
(in percentages)

		The Groups			
Proposed Consequences	Polk-Metro *High* N = 132	San Pablo *Parochial* 166	Makai *High* 31	Pele *C.C.* 24	Northcoast *Univers.* 63	Saudi *Arabia* 126
Case 3: Drug Dealing and Stabbing a Teacher						
Detention for:						
1 year	71	74	63	83	48	53
Less than a year	.3	3			6	
Probation	24	8	19	8	6	12
Counseling	3	5		33	41	
Sent to School	5	5	13	13	14	12
Foster Home	.3	.2		13	14	
Case 4: Radio Theft and Striking a Policeman						
Detention for:						
1 year	35	46	38	46	32	13
Less than a year		4			11	
Probation	42	51	50	50	40	83
Counseling	1	14	16	38	33	
Sent to School	60	51	50	50	46	83
Foster Home	58	54	50	50	49	83
Pay Victim's Medical Costs		4			8	

2. Was the level of severity of sanctions consistent from one case of wrong-doing to another?

3. To what extent did the members within each group agree on how severe the consequences should be?

Overall Severity Level

The general level of severity for a group on any of the six cases was estimated by inspecting the percentage of respondents in each group who, for each case, recommended the sanction that (a) was most painful and/or (b) placed the greatest restriction on an offender's freedom to live life in whatever way that he or she chose. For each case of wrongdoing, the percentages of these most-severe sanctions are listed in Table 6-6 for the six groups. As shown by the final item in the table, the average severity percentages across all six cases were nearly the same (40% to 45%) for all groups except the Northcoast University graduate students (30%), who were visibly more lenient than the others in their proposed consequences (although the difference between Northcoast and others exceeded a

Table 6-4

Group Comparisons — Cases 5 & 6
(in percentages)

	The Groups					
Proposed Consequences	Polk-Metro *High*	San Pablo *Parochial*	Makai *High*	Pele *C.C.*	Northcoast *Univers.*	Saudi *Arabia*
	N = 132	*166*	*31*	*24*	*63*	*126*
Case 5: Driving After Drinking						
Jail for:						
1 year	34	51	34	25	14	42
Less than a year	5	18		8	3	
Pay Victims'						
Medical Costs	66	62	75	63	33	43
Pay $1,000 Fine	55	51	72	54	41	43
Driver's License						
Revoked	16	36	28	46	12	5
Counseling	.3	8	6	13	6	
Community Service		1		21	10	
Case 6: Driving While Medicated						
Jail for:						
1 year	20	20	22	12	11	25
Less than a year	.3	9			4	
Pay Victims'						
Medical Costs	70	75	66	63	33	56
Pay $1,000 Fine	69	70	59	58	30	56
Driver's License						
Revoked	11	31	13	20	22	12
Community Service		2		13	10	

.05 level of significance only in the cases of Polk-Metro and San Pablo). In all six cases fewer Northcoast students selected the most severe consequence than did students in the other groups (with the single exception of the Saudi Arabians' proposal for the teenage boy).

In an effort to understand the reasons for such a pattern, we speculated that a combination of two factors—age and vocational motivation—might account for the less severe sanctions recommended by Northcoast teacher-training students. The Northcoast respondents, whose mean age was 32 years, were on the average 7 to 17 years older than members of the other five groups. Thus, the Northcoast participants had spent more time viewing life's events from an adult perspective. Furthermore, as explained in Chapter 2, many of the Northcoast students had already been engaged in an occupation and were now returning to school to seek a second or sometimes a third career. Some said they had become disillusioned with the business world and hence were turning to teaching as a way of working with young people and "touching the future." In their answers to the opinionnaire questions, many of them criticized harsh consequences as devices for simply punishing offenders rather than furnishing opportunities for wrongdoers to reform. This perspective, favoring rehabilitation over punishment, was in keeping with the attitudes toward learners that the instructors in the Northcoast program were seeking to promote among their teacher-education candidates.

When we originally selected groups to participate in the opinionnaire survey, we searched for ones whose social environments might foster significantly different moral values. For example, we estimated that the high incidence of inner-city crime and poverty of the Polk-Metro district might provide a notably different moral climate than did the social environment experienced by students attending San Pablo Parochial High or by those in the Saudi Arabian institutions. Furthermore, the two groups in Hawaii probably had a still different set of environmental conditions helping shape their moral attitudes. However, as Table 6-6 indicates, we were wrong in expecting these diverse social settings to be associated with different overall levels of consequence severity that respondents would propose. Except for the Northcoast University students, the other five groups appeared nearly alike in how harsh they might generally be in their treatment of wrongdoers.

Consistency of Severity Across Cases

If respondents were completely consistent from one case to another in the severity of the sanctions they chose, then we might expect each column in Table 6-6 to display the same percentage from case 1 through case 6. Not only might 55% of Polk-Metro students recommend the death penalty for the army colonel, but 55% would also recommend the most severe sanction in each of the other cases as well. However, as figures in the table show, there are marked differences from one case to another in the proportion of respondents suggesting a severe consequence.

The most dramatic inconsistency is seen in the Saudi Arabians' proposals for the Nazi major and for the boy who stole the car radio. Whereas 72% would put the major to death, only 13% would place the boy in a detention facility. As shown in Table 6-3, rather than incarcerating the boy, 83% of the Saudi Arabians would place him in a foster home and in school under the supervision of a probation officer. One possible explanation for the harsh punishment of the major and the more lenient treatment of the boy is that in Saudi Arabian tradition murder and illicit drug trade have both warranted an extremely aversive response, while disobedience among the young has been corrected principally within a strong family structure.

Nearly as dramatic is the discrepancy in how severely Polk-Metro and San Pablo students would treat the girl who sold drugs as compared to the woman who drove while medicated. Over 70% (Table 6-3) of Polk-Metro and San Pablo respondents would incarcerate the girl for a year, but only 20% (Table 6-4) would jail the woman for that length of time. In effect, high school students in a crime-ridden urban center and those in a more tranquil small city both appeared to apply similar values to this pair of cases. The girl was judged so out of control that she should be removed from society for an extended period, whereas the woman was not such a public threat and could be allowed her freedom so long as she paid a fine and the accident victim's medical expenses.

Table 6-5

Statistically   Significant   Differences
(in percentages)

Proposed Consequence	*Higher % Group*	*Lower % Group*	*Statistically Significant*
Case 1: Ordering Partisans' Executions			
Death	Polk-Metro (55)	San Pablo (32)	.001
	Polk-Metro (55)	Northcoast (40)	.05
	Polk-Metro (55)	Saudi Arabia (40)	.05
Set Free	San Pablo (25)	Northcoast (6)	.001
	Makai (28)	Northcoast (6)	.05
	Makai (28)	Polk-Metro (13)	.01
	San Pablo (25)	Polk-Metro (13)	.01
	Pele (42)	Polk-Metro (13)	.01
Case 2: Supervising Partisans' Executions			
Death	Saudi Arabia (72)	Pele (33)	.001
	Saudi Arabia (72)	Polk-Metro (54)	.01
	Polk-Metro (54)	Pele (33)	.05
	Makai (63)	Pele (33)	.05
	Makai (63)	San Pablo (44)	.05
Prison	Polk-Metro (43)	Saudi Arabia (16)	.001
	Northcoast (46)	Saudi Arabia (16)	.001
	San Pablo (43)	Saudi Arabia (16)	.001
Case 3: Drug Dealing and Stabbing a Teacher			
1-yr. Detention	San Pablo (74)	Northcoast (48)	.001
	Pele (83)	Northcoast (48)	.001
	Polk-Metro (71)	Northcoast (48)	.01
	Pele (83)	Saudi Arabia (53)	.001
	Polk-Metro (71)	Saudi Arabia (53)	.01
Probation	Polk-Metro (24)	San Pablo (8)	.001
	Polk-Metro (24)	Northcoast (6)	.001
	Polk-Metro (24)	Pele (8)	.01
	Polk-Metro (24)	Saudi Arabia (12)	.05
Counseling	Northcoast (41)	Polk-Metro (3)	.001
	Northcoast (41)	San Pablo (5)	.001
	Pele (33)	Polk-Metro (3)	.01
	Pele (33)	San Pablo (5)	.01

It can be noted as well that the amount of agreement between two groups often varied from one case to another. Whereas nearly the same proportion of Polk-Metro (71%) and San Pablo (74%) students agreed on sending the girl to a detention center (Table 6-3), more than half (55%) of Polk-Metro respondents

Table 6-5 continued

Statistically Significant Differences
(in percentages)

Proposed Consequence	*Higher % Group*	*Lower % Group*	*Statistically Significant*
Case 4: Radio Theft and Striking a Policeman			
1-yr. Detention	US Groups (32-46)	Saudi Arabia (13)	.01-.001
Probation	Saudi Arabia (83)	US Groups (40-51)	.01-.001
Foster Home	Saudi Arabia (83)	US Groups (46-58)	.01-.001
Case 5: Driving After Drinking			
1-year Jail	San Pablo (51)	Northcoast (14)	.001
	San Pablo (51)	Polk-Metro (34)	.01
	San Pablo (51)	Makai (34)	.01
	San Pablo (51)	Pele (25)	.01
	Saudi Arabia (42)	Northcoast (14)	.001
Medical Costs	Polk-Metro (66)	Northcoast (33)	.001
	San Pablo (62)	Northcoast (33)	.001
	Makai (75)	Northcoast (33)	.001
	Pele (63)	Northcoast (33)	.01
	Polk-Metro (66)	Saudi Arabia (43)	.001
	Makai (75)	Saudi Arabia (43)	.001
	San Pablo (62)	Saudi Arabia (43)	.01
$1000 Fine	Makai (72)	Northcoast (41)	.01
	Makai (72)	Saudi Arabia (43)	.01
	Makai (72)	San Pablo (51)	.05
Revoke License	San Pablo (36)	Polk-Metro (16)	.001
	San Pablo (36)	Saudi Arabia (5)	.001
	Pele (46)	Saudi Arabia (5)	.001
	Pele (46)	Polk-Metro (16)	.01
	Pele (46)	Northcoast (12)	.01
	Polk-Metro (16)	Saudi Arabia (5)	.01
Case 6: Driving While Medicated			
Medical Costs	5 others)56-75)	Northcoast (33)	.05-.001
	San Pablo (75)	Saudi Arabia (56)	.01
	Saudi Arabia (56)	Northcoast (33)	.01
$1000 Fine	5 Others (56-70)	Northcoast (30)	.01-.001
Revoke License	San Pablo (31)	Polk-Metro (11)	.001

would execute the army major while less than one-third (32%) of San Pablo students would do so (Table 6-2). In contrast, barely one-third (34%) of Polk-Metro students would jail the drinking driver, whereas more than half (51%) of San Pablo students would lock him up (Table 6-4). In trying to account for this difference, we might speculate that driving under the influence of alcohol was perhaps more common and thereby considered less serious in the Polk-Metro community than in the small city of Vista Verde where San Pablo students lived.

This phenomenon of inconsistency across cases is illustrated in greater detail in Tables 6-2 through 6-5. Lack of consistency is found not only with the most severe sanctions, but with the other common types of consequences as well. For instance, most Pele Community College students (83%) would detain the girl who sold drugs, but less than half (46%) would do so to the boy who stole the car radio (Table 6-3). Likewise, nearly half (48%) of Northcoast University respondents would place the girl in detention but hardly a third (32%) would detain the boy (Table 6-3).

In summary, there is marked inconsistency across cases in the severity of consequences proposed by different groups. This inconsistency seems to result from the patterns of moral values that dominate within the particular group. The results reported in the foregoing tables can serve as a warning to people who are

Table 6-6

The Severity Level of Consequences
(in percentages)

The Cases	*The Groups*					
	Polk-Metro High	*San Pablo Parochial*	*Makai High*	*Pele C.C.*	*Northcoast Univers.*	*Saudi Arabia*
Army Colonel Death	55	32	38	42	40	40
Army Major Death	54	44	63	33	37	72
Girl —Drug Sale 1-Year Detention	71	74	63	83	48	53
Boy —Radio Theft 1-Year Detention	35	46	38	46	32	13
Drinking Driver 1-Year in Jail	34	51	34	25	14	42
Medicated Driver 1-Year in Jail	20	20	22	12	11	25
Average of All Cases Combined	45	45	43	40	30	41

prone to use a group's proposed consequences in one case as the basis for estimating the consequences that group will recommend in other cases that involve somewhat different conditions. Apparently it is the complex and somewhat individualistic configurations of people's moral values that renders attempts at generalizing across cases quite hazardous.

Within-Group Consistency

Tables 6-2, 6-3, and 6-4 provide evidence about how much the members within each group agreed on proposed consequences. To judge intragroup agreement we used the following criteria:

> A high level of agreement obtains whenever (a) a high percentage of respondents choose the same consequence and (b) the number of different consequences is very small. A low level of agreement obtains whenever (a) no single consequence is chosen by a large percentage of respondents and (b) the respondents' choices are distributed over a wide variety of consequences.

A total of 148 consequence choices appear in Tables 6-2, 6-3, and 6-4. To show the overall extent of agreement within groups for the entire array of percentages in the tables, we have summarized the data in terms of levels of agreement by group. The left column in Table 6-7 lists percentage categories. Figures in the body of the table indicate the number of times that a group's choice fell within each of the percentage categories. For example, in only one instance did as many as 80% of Pele Community College students agree with each other on a sanction. In only three instances did as many as 70% to 79% of San Pablo students agree on a choice.

As the totals in the far right column show, in only 33 instances did at least 50% of the members in a group agree on the choice of a consequence. In the remaining 115 instances, less than half of the respondents in a group agreed on a sanction. As we consider these data, we should recall that Tables 6-2, 6-3, and 6-4 list only those consequences that were proposed by at least 2% of any group's members. Missing from the tables are numbers of other consequences that were selected by a very few respondents. Within some groups as many as 15% of the respondents offered individualistic, rarely-cited options. Therefore, the extent of disagreement within groups was actually greater than the data in Table 6-7 indicate.

A conclusion we have drawn from the foregoing analysis is that, among the members of any group that participated in the present study, there was no consensus about which consequences are most suitable for wrongdoers in the kinds of cases that participants were asked to judge. Consequently, it is a very risky venture to use the sanction proposed by one group member—or even by a few members—as the basis for predicting the sanctions that other members of that group will propose. The percentages in Tables 6-2 through 6-7 suggest that, in terms of moral decisions, certain members of one of our groups were more like a substantial number of students in the other groups than they were like other members of their own group.

Table 6-7

Within-Group Agreement on Consequences
(in numbers of instances)

	The Groups						
Percentage Categories	*Polk-Metro High*	*San Pablo Parochial*	*Makai High*	*Pele C.C.*	*Northcoast Univers.*	*Saudi Arabia*	*Total*
80-89%			1			3	4
70-79%	2	3	2			1	8
60-69%	2	1	3	2			8
50-59%	3	2	2	3		3	13
40-49%	2	3		3	6	4	18
30-39%	3	4	4	2	6		19
20-29%	2	2	5	5	1	2	17
10-19%	3	2	4	5	9	6	29
0-9%	9	12	1	2	7	1	32

Initiative in Proposing Consequences

In the following discussion, we are using the term *initiative* to identify the degree to which participants in this study created a consequence of their own to apply to wrongdoers rather than selecting one of the options listed below the cases on the opinionnaire. Groups proposing a higher percentage of consequences of their own invention are credited with a higher level of initiative, creativity, and independence of thought than are groups proposing a lower percentage.

Levels of initiative displayed by the five American groups are provided in Table 6-8. Our method of computing a group's initiative percentage for a case consisted of dividing the number of nonlisted, respondent-devised consequences by the total number of consequences cited in that case. Some respondents proposed only one consequence per case. Others, however, recommended a combination of two or more sanctions. As a result, the total number of consequences cited in a given case exceeded the number of respondents. For instance, in the example of the boy who stole the car stereo, the 166 San Pablo students offered a total of 397 consequences. Sixty-two of those 397 were ones devised by the students themselves rather than selected from the options below the case. Dividing 62 by 397 produced the 16% initiative percentage that appears in Table 6-8. (Data for Saudi Arabian students are not included in the table, since the 15% of students in that group who checked the option labeled "other" under each case did not specify what that "other" option would be.)

As shown by the bottom line in Table 6-8, the lowest level of initiative was exhibited by the inner-city high school students (4.4%) and the highest degree by the university teacher-education candidates (32.9%). In other words, participants

Table 6-8

Frequency of Non-Listed Consequences
(in percentages)

The Cases	*Polk-Metro High*	*San Pablo Parochial*	*Makai High*	*Pele C.C.*	*Northcoast University*
1. Army Colonel	6	16	6	20	27
2. Army Major	4	11	9	38	23
3. Girl —Drug Sale	9	25	13	36	62
4. Boy —Radio Theft	3	16	12	20	32
5. Drinking Driver	4	14	3	23	23
6. Medicated Driver	3	7	2	13	12
Cases 1-6 Combined	4.4	14.3	7.1	19.1	32.9

at Northcoast University created their own consequences nearly eight times more often than did students at Polk-Metro High. Respondents at San Pablo Parochial high school on the West Coast (14.3%) invented sanctions twice as often as did students at Makai High in Hawaii (7.1%). The community college participants produced their own consequences in somewhat greater numbers (19.1) than did the parochial high school students. Not only did these trends obtain over the six cases combined, but they appeared in the same order in nearly all of the individual cases as well.

The tendency to create new options rather than choose from those listed below a case description was greatest for the misdeeds of the two teenagers, and it was most pronounced in the incident of the girl who had sold drugs and stabbed the teacher. In these two cases, the apparent reason for respondents' dissatisfaction with the listed alternatives was that they felt they could conceive of more constructive treatments than those in the listed options for rehabilitating adolescents who seemed to be on the road to a life of crime.

During the process of scoring opinionnaire answers, our attention was drawn to differences among the respondent groups in their ability to communicate their ideas in writing. Therefore, we devised a way to estimate the levels of English-language competence reflected in the rationales that respondents wrote in support of their suggested consequences. Our estimate of competence was based on the correctness of the grammar, syntax, punctuation, and spelling of students' written opinions. Another feature of the rationales that perhaps was indicative of students' command of English was the amount they wrote. In our estimation, a variable entitled *length of written comments* was likely determined by two main factors, only one of which was language competence. We speculated that the length of rationales could result from either (a) the individuals' fertility of ideas in support of a suggested consequence and/or (b) the ease with which respondents could explain their ideas in writing. We judged that at least part of the reason some students wrote very little was that they felt constrained by their lack of fluency in written expression.

It was not possible to assess the language skills of the Saudi Arabian students, because rarely did any of them add comments to their consequence suggestions, and those few comments were in Arabic, not English. However, as indicated in Table 6-9, the five American groups could be compared on written-language ability. The comparison was based on a random sample of 10 opinionnaires from each of the five groups. With six cases per questionnaire, this meant that an assessment of a group's writing competence was derived from the analysis of students' comments under 60 cases. The phrase "average words per case" refers to how much students wrote beneath a case in defense of their proposed consequence. The computation of "one error per how many words" was performed by dividing the total number of words produced by a group by the total number of writing errors.

Among the five American groups, the written-language results at Makai High and Polk-Metro were nearly identical. Those schools' students wrote the least and made the most errors per amount of writing. Although participants from Pele College wrote somewhat more than the ones at San Pablo High, those two groups were much the same in the frequency of their errors. The largest amount of writing per case and the fewest errors were found among the graduate students at Northcoast University. They wrote 150% more than did respondents at Makai and Polk-Metro and committed hardly 16% of the total of the high school students' mistakes.

Such results do not seem surprising. Students at both Makai and Polk-Metro lived in communities in which daily discourse was conducted in language that did not match the style of English approved in school. Residents in the Makai area commonly used an amount of Hawaii Creole (pidgin) English, and ones in the Polk-Metro district frequently employed an inner-city patois and Spanish. Youths from such language settings could be expected to express themselves less adequately in writing so-called standard English than would students attending San Pablo High, where families were of a higher socioeconomic status and accustomed to communicating in a form of English closer to the school standard. Furthermore, observations of typical instructional methods at Polk-Metro showed that students were seldom assigned writing tasks or expected to propose

Table 6-9
Language Competence of Group Members

The Group	Average Words per Case	One Error per How Many Words?
Makai High	15	9
Polk-Metro High	16	8
San Pablo Parochial High	26	22
Pele Community College	32	21
Northcoast University	39	56

analyses of complex social situations. Such was not the case at San Pablo High. Finally, we might readily expect the best performance on the part of Northcoast University's graduate students who were preparing to be teachers.

In summary, from the viewpoint of independence of thought in proposing consequences, respondents who were older and further advanced in the formal-education hierarchy displayed greater initiative than those who were younger and lower in the hierarchy. Furthermore, respondents whose daily language environment was closer to the standard advocated in the typical American school displayed a higher level of initiative; wrote at greater length in defense of consequence recommendations; and committed fewer grammar, spelling, and syntax errors.

In an effort to identify the reasons behind the contrasts among groups in initiative and written-language skill, we speculated that such differences resulted from three main factors: (1) variations in innate aptitude, (2) types of learning experiences, and (3) selection.

The phrase *innate aptitude* refers to the potential sensitivity and complexity of the human nervous system as derived from an individual's genetic composition. In effect, we assume that acuity of sight and hearing, speed and accuracy of perception, efficiency of memory storage and retrieval, skill in combining disparate stimuli and memories to form complicated concepts, and adeptness in expressing ideas in speech and writing will all depend to some degree on the nature of the individual's inherited neural equipment. We assume as well that the rate at which such competencies develop as a person grows up also depends to some extent on genetic endowment. People more favored in innate neural potential have a better chance of profiting from learning experiences, and thus of exhibiting greater initiative and language skill, than do people less favored.

As for learning experiences, we suggest that environments within which children and youth develop can differ in the kinds of moral-decision events available and in the ways mentors guide youngsters' mental processing of those events. In other words, we assume that the moral values individuals adopt are strongly influenced by the kinds of moral events they witness and by the attitudes and teaching methods of their mentors (parents, siblings, teachers, religious leaders, peers, mass-communication media, and the like).

The term *selection* in the present context alludes to the weeding-out or winnowing function of the typical formal-education hierarchy. As students advance to the upper rungs of the education ladder, those less successful in academic pursuits either are pushed out or else they drop out of their own accord. Those who remain in the system are ones who have proven more adept at oral and written communication, at grasping complex concepts, and at analyzing the complicated issues that make up so much of advanced academic content. Therefore, not only is the population of higher-education institutions composed of a select, academically adept segment of youths and young adults, but the daily learning tasks of such people involve analyzing and synthesizing complex issues. In other words, this select group regularly engages in guided opportunities to produce reasoned value judgments.

We are, therefore, suggesting that the individual and group differences in initiative and English-language skill observed in the present investigation might be accounted for by the interaction of the foregoing three variables. Within a particular group the observed differences among group members could result from individual differences in the members' neural endowment and learning experiences. Differences between two groups of students who are about the same age—such as the Polk-Metro and San Pablo samples—may result more from differences in environmental learning opportunities than from the group members' innate neural potentials. Differences between the high school and university samples likely result from a combination of all three factors, as the selective function of the educational hierarchy serves to populate graduate schools with students who are the product of both favored innate neural potential and favored learning opportunities. In addition, part of the graduate students' favored learning opportunities is likely a function of age. The Northcoast students were considerably older than the members of the high-school groups and consequently had accumulated more years of learning opportunities from which to profit.

CONCLUSION

The data analyzed in this chapter appear to support the following observations about the types of consequences people apply to offenders in described incidents of wrongdoing.

1. When asked to suggest consequences for offenders:
   a. Most people will select one or more of the consequence options that accompany the case descriptions rather than create consequences of their own.
   b. Older respondents who have progressed higher up the schooling ladder will more often devise their own consequences than will younger respondents who are lower in the educational hierarchy.
2. Even though only a small minority of the respondents (perhaps 10% to 15%) create their own consequence proposals, the types of sanctions and treatments offered by that minority can be quite numerous and diverse.
3. The level of severity of consequences recommended by respondents will vary from one case to another, depending on conditions in the different cases and on the pattern of values that respondents bring to their judgments of the cases. Therefore, only at a considerable risk of error can we use a group's consequence proposals in one case as the basis for predicting the consequences that members of a group will apply to another case whose conditions are somewhat different. In brief, there is likely to be substantial inconsistency from case to case in the severity of sanctions respondents recommend.
4. Among the types of groups that participated in the present study, the amount of variability among the members of a given group in the kinds of consequences they would propose is likely to be greater than the variation between the majority of one group and the majority of another group. In other words, the similarity of opinion patterns across groups appears to be greater than the similarity of opinions among members within a group. Therefore, in most instances, knowing the consequence a particular person recommends in a given case is not a trustworthy guide to identifying the

group from which that person comes. This suggests that stereotyping individuals and groups in terms of the consequences they are expected to propose for wrongdoing is an activity involving high risk.

The above generalizations can be viewed as hypotheses that await refinement and testing with people from social environments and age categories different from those of the groups in the present study.

7

Moral Principles and Conditions Affecting Their Application

As explained in Chapter 3, moral principles are beliefs people hold about right and wrong ways to behave toward others. In addition, many people apply moral principles to relationships between humans and such supernatural forces as gods or the spirits of dead ancestors. Some also employ principles as the basis for the treatment of animals and such features of the environment as art objects, physical possessions, plants, mountains, or bodies of water.

In Chapter 3 we contended that principles are seldom, if ever, applied in exactly the same way to every moral-decision situation. Instead, how a given principle will be used is typically influenced by certain conditions that obtain in the particular moral incident at hand. Conditions, in effect, are characteristics of people or of their environment that affect the way principles are interpreted for determining the consequences wrongdoers should face.

Chapter 7 describes the place of principles and conditions in the rationales that 416 opinionnaire respondents offered when defending the consequences they proposed for transgressors in the six cases of wrongdoing. (Because the 126 Saudi Arabian students who took part in the survey did not offer rationales, the material in this chapter is founded on the results of the 416 respondents from the other five groups whose opinions were sought.) The chapter opens with a description of principles implied in opinionnaire responses, continues with a report of conditions, and closes with an assessment of the adequacy of opinionnaire and interview approaches to discovering the principles and conditions people bring to cases of wrongdoing.

PRINCIPLES BEHIND CONSEQUENCE RECOMMENDATIONS

Because people rarely stated outright the principles on which they based their moral decisions, it was necessary to infer those principles from proposed consequences and supporting rationales. To guide our effort in identifying principles, we adopted four rules of inference:

1. Whenever behavior in a moral incident is judged to be improper, the impropriety can be interpreted as the violation of a moral principle whose nature is reflected in that misbehavior.

   Examples of the principle: *Do not inflict physical injury on others.*
   "He ordered the execution of all those Yugoslavs."
   "She stabbed the teacher."
   "He smacked the cop in the face with a pipe."

2. Whenever a consequence is recommended for a person in a moral incident, and the consequence is intended to <u>correct misbehavior</u>, the principle that was violated may be inferred from the rationale offered in defense of that consequence.

   Examples of the principle: *Respect the law.*
   "Having his driver's license taken away should teach him to obey the drunk-driving law in the future."
   "The Yugoslav agents were operating illegally when they kidnapped the army major in South America, so the major should go free."

3. Whenever the consequence in a moral incident is intended to <u>ameliorate the damaging effect of the wrongdoing</u>, the principle that was violated can be inferred from the nature of the consequence.

   Examples of the principle: *Show compassion for victims of wrongdoing.*
   "The motorist should pay the injured boy's medical bills."
   "The former Nazi major's property should be confiscated and the proceeds divided among the living relatives of the executed Yugoslavs."

4. The rationale supporting a recommended consequence may identify the essence of the principle on which the recommendation is founded.

   Examples of the principle: *Fulfill obligations incurred by choice or by the nature of one's role in life.*
   "She was being irresponsible by driving after taking the medicine."
   "It was the major's duty to carry out the orders of his superior officer."

From our analysis of opinionnaires, we concluded that 22 of the 30 moral principles described in Chapter 3 could be inferred from one or more of the 416 respondents' answers. However, only the 11 principles displayed in Table 7-1 were applied by more than 1% of the respondents. Each of the remaining 11 was implied by less than 1% of the participants. (The 8 principles not applied in any of the six cases of misdeeds are identified by asterisks in Chapter 3.)

To understand the way we employed the rules of inference, consider first why we judged that 100% of the respondents applied two of the moral principles in all six cases. The two principles—identified in the table as *punish wrongdoing* and *physical well-being*—were defined in Chapter 3 as:

Reformation of Misbehavior: The proper response to wrongdoing is to submit the offender to a type of treatment that will result in a reformation so he or she will behave morally in the future.

Punishment of Misbehavior: Every act of misbehavior should be retaliated with punishment.

Concern for Human Life —Physical: Everyone should protect others from physical harm.

Disregard for Human Life: No one should exploit or harm others physically.

The line of reasoning that led us to such a judgment derived from three assumptions: (1) that all respondents believed there had been wrongdoing, (2) that the wrongdoing involved physical injury (*concern for human life*), and (3) that something should be done about the person who had caused the injury (*treatment/punishment*).

Some respondents made clear in their supporting rationales that the central misdeed in each case was that of harming someone. Their belief that a principle of physical well-being had been violated was reflected in such phrases as "The driver put two women in the hospital" and "The colonel's order ended the lives of more than 100 people." However, many others gave no direct indication of which kind of wrongdoing they believed a case represented, yet we were assuming from their proposed sanctions (inference rule 1) that a principle of physical well-being had been the foundation of their proposal. We tested this assumption in our 20 interviews by asking: "Was there any wrongdoing in this case that we just read? And if so, what was the wrongdoing?" In every instance the interviewees identified *inflicting physical injury* as the misdeed. Hence, we accepted this evidence as confirming that 100% of the opinionnaire respondents apparently believed that a principle of physical well-being had been violated in the six cases. (In the instances of the Nazi major and the high school girl, drug dealing was also cited as wrongdoing. In addition, the teenage boy's stealing the car radio and the male motorist's driving under the influence of alcohol were identified as misdeeds.)

Most of the people we interviewed seemed amazed that we asked them to state which kinds of transgressions were committed in the six cases. This display of surprise appeared to support the observation that principles that proscribe killing, theft, and the distribution of harmful drugs are such universal, deeply ingrained cultural values that it is unnecessary—perhaps even ridiculous—to ask that they be specified. Apparently, as children mature into adulthood, the socialization process they experience embeds such moral principles so thoroughly into their belief systems that the question of which moral values were violated in our six cases did not even need to be asked. In the present study, the younger respondents in particular tended to assume that the values on which they founded their consequences were too obvious to mention.

In Table 7-1, the remaining principles that were not scored at 100% were rated on the basis of the contents of rationales that participants included in defense of their recommended consequences. Judgments of rationales were guided by inference rules 2, 3, and 4. The analysis showed that the issue of which principles are applied in a case depends not only on the type of transgression involved but also on personal characteristics of the transgressors or of the victims of wrongdoing. For example, more respondents expressed compassion for the transgressor in the case of the homeless teenage radio thief than for the aged and ill army colonel or for the girl who sold drugs and knifed the teacher. As another instance, a higher percentage of respondents censured the two errant motorists for irresponsibility than cited the offenders in the other cases for not behaving responsibly. It also appeared that listing a consequence option beneath a case increased the likelihood that respondents would adopt a moral principle implied in that sanction. For instance, compassion fo the victims of the auto

Table 7-1

Moral Principles Implied in the Six Cases
(in percentages, N=416)

	The Cases					
Type of Principle	*Army Colonel*	*Army Major*	*Girl & Drugs*	*Boy & Stereo*	*Drinking Driver*	*Medicated Driver*
—*General Social Obligations*—						
Punish Wrongdoing	100	100	100	100	100	100
Responsibility	2	1	2	1	12	12
Respect for Right		1	2			
Respect for the Law	1	2		1	1	1
Protection of Society	6	6	4	2	6	3
Even-Handed Justice	1					
—*Affective Regard for Others*—						
Physical Well-Being	100	100	100	100	100	100
Compassion: Victim	5	4	5	4	31	37
Compassion: Wrongdoer	24	6	29	49	6	9
—*Personal Rights*—						
Self-Preservation	1			4		
Reasonable Punishment	2	1				

accidents was reflected in the option that required the motorists to pay the medical expenses of the people they had injured. However, under the other four cases, no option was listed that would provide reparations to victims of the misdeeds; so it was necessary for respondents to create such an option if they wished to compensate victims in those incidents.

In an effort to discover if the five respondent groups differed significantly from each other in the moral principles they applied to the cases, we compared the groups on each principle. The comparison showed that, with few exceptions, the groups were all quite similar in their judgments. In other words, the percentage of members in a group who implied a given principle in a case was nearly the same across groups. One noteworthy exception was found in the incident of the girl who sold drugs; significantly more (.01) Northcoast University students (46%) applied the principle of *compassion for the offender* than did students from the three high schools—San Pablo (30%), Polk-Metro (27%), and Makai (10%). Another exception appeared in the case of the boy who stole the car stereo; significantly fewer (.001) Polk-Metro students (30%) expressed compassion for the boy than did respondents from San Pablo (66%), Makai (52%), and Northcoast University (52%). In effect, the Northcoast teacher-education candidates generally displayed greater compassion for teenagers who engaged in delinquent acts than did the inner-city Polk-Metro students. In seeking to account for this difference, we speculated that the adults preparing for the teaching profession had more faith in rehabilitating adolescents through education, counseling, and foster-family care than did the youths attending Polk-Metro High. As another possibility, students in the Polk-Metro community perhaps were more accustomed to the jailing of wrongdoers than to attempts at more positive efforts toward reforming delinquent youth.

One other notable difference among the groups was seen in the percentage of students who expressed compassion for the former German army colonel by either sentencing him to a shorter prison term or setting him free. In this case it was the San Pablo Parochial High School students (39%) who were significantly (.01) more lenient in their recommendations than were students from Polk-Metro (14%), Makai (19%), Pele College (13%), or Northcoast University (10%). This difference may have been the result of a greater proportion of San Pablo respondents believing that the peacetime proscription against killing did not apply in wartime and that the colonel deserved credit for having become a law-abiding citizen since the war. In brief, conditions in each case could affect the way a given principle was interpreted for purposes of recommending consequences, which brings us to the analysis of the conditions themselves.

THE DIVERSITY AND FREQUENCY OF CONDITIONS

Conditions affecting the application of principles in specific cases were often included in the replies students wrote to explain why they considered their suggested consequences suitable. Each of the 44 conditions described in Chapter 3 was cited at least once among the 416 respondents' rationales, so that the types of conditions that influenced respondents' proposals were numerous and quite diverse.

In contrast to moral principles, conditions were frequently stated outright rather than merely implied. For example, numbers of respondents defended their lenient treatment of the former Nazi colonel by stating, "He's now very old and sick, and he's led a law-abiding life all these years since the war." Such a rationale was credited with including three of the postincident circumstances delineated in Chapter 3—the wrongdoer's age, health status, and reformation. However, not all participants identified conditions so directly. As a result, scoring some conditions required a measure of inference. For instance, the phrase "He's just a kid, so they shouldn't go too hard on him" was scored under the category *Undue Burden*, a condition defined as "The proposed consequence would be an unreasonable burden for the offender to bear."

The 25 conditions that were applied by 2% or more of the respondents are listed in Table 7-2. Less than 2% of the participants cited each of the remaining 19 conditions not included in the table. The figures within the table report the percentage of students in the sample of 416 that acknowledged a given condition. The term *acknowledged* here means that a condition was mentioned or implied in a respondent's rationale, with the mention assuming any one of three forms. That is, in acknowledging a condition, a participant could:

1. Say that the condition warranted a more lenient consequence.
   Personal Problems: "The boy was homeless and in obvious psychological distress, so he should have counseling and guidance instead of just being locked up."

Reformation vs. Recidivism: "The colonel had become a good citizen and deserves to go free."

Elapsed Time: "The war was a long time ago. I don't see any point in prosecuting the army officer now. It's best to let bygones be bygones."

2. Say that the condition warranted a more aversive consequence.

Reformation vs. Recidivism: "The major was still committing crimes by engaging in illegal drug sales, so he deserves to be put to death."

Major vs. Minor Harm: "If the girl had just been selling a little pot, she could be put on probation, but stabbing the teacher means she'd better beput in juvenile hall for a year."

Redeeming Reason vs. Inexcusable Violation: "With all the publicity about the dangers of drunk driving, everybody knows it's wrong. The man had no excuse for drinking and then getting behind the wheel. A year in jail will keep him off the streets and should teach him a lesson."

3. Say that the condition should have no effect on the decision about what sanctions to impose.

Personal Problems: "Being poor is no reason to go around knifing people."

Elapsed Time: "Even though many years have passed since the colonel ordered the execution of the Yugoslavians, he still should pay the price for committing murder."

The following examples illustrate ways that various combinations of the three forms of acknowledgment might appear in different cases. Among the 9% of respondents who acknowledged the condition *personal problems* in the case of the girl who sold marijuana, 3% said her problems warranted leniency, whereas 6% said her problems had no bearing on the sanctions she should face. Among the 23% who cited the condition *reformation vs. recidivism* in the case of the former Nazi major, 15% said his postwar criminal behavior called for stringent sanctions, whereas 8% said his behavior since World War II should have no influence on the consequences imposed by the Yugoslav court. All 11% of those who referred to *major harm vs. minor harm* in the case of the drinking driver cited that condition as support for imposing strict punishment on the offender.

To summarize, people can be motivated by any one of three intentions when they allude to conditions in a case of wrongdoing. Their intention may be (a) to reinforce a recommendation for leniency, (b) to buttress a recommendation of strict punishment, or (c) to emphasize that the condition should exert no influence on the decision about consequences.

Of the 57 percentages reported in the table, 43 are less than 10%, 9 range from 10% to 19%, and only 5 are as high as 20%. More than two dozen other percentages do not appear in the table because they were less than 2% each. Such a large quantity of small percentages suggests that there was relatively little agreement among respondents about which conditions were worthy of mention. In other words, the dominant trend was for respondents to display diverse, individualistic opinions rather than expressing the same views as their fellow group members.

Furthermore, the kinds of conditions that respondents viewed as important varied from one type of case to another. The only variable that at least 2% of respondents considered important across all cases was that of *major vs. minor harm*. Each of the remaining conditions was judged important in some cases but

Table 7-2

Conditions Cited or Implied in the Six Cases
(in percentages, N = 416)

Type of Condition	Army Colonel	Army Major	Girl & Drugs	Boy & Stereo	Drinking Driver	Medicated Driver
—Character Traits—						
Good vs. Bad Character	3	2		3		
Redeeming Reason vs. Inexcusable Violation			3			
Know Right & Wrong			3		10	19
—Prior Circumstances—						
Inadequate Social Support			19	26		
—Concurrent Circumstances—						
Personal Problems			9	4	10	
Reasonable Risk					3	17
Role Suitability	5	6				
Duress vs. Volition	3	4				
Age of Offender			6	4		
Extenuating Circumstances				4	2	3
Suspension of Rules	4					
Loss of Inhibition			4			7
Misperception of Situation						2
—Post-Incident Circumstances—						
State of Health	24	2				
Age of Offender	16					
Reformation vs. Recidivism	11	23				
Elapsed Time	13	3				
Reparation Opportunity			2			2
Repentance vs. Impenitence	2					
—Fair Chance—						
Self-Improvement Opportunity			9	8		
Second Chance			2	3	3	
Likelihood of Improvement				3	2	
—Extent of Damage—						
Major vs. Minor Harm	20	21	9	4	11	4
Potential Harm				3	5	3
—Legal Considerations—						
Legal vs. Illegal Act	3			3	4	3

Note: Conditions cited by fewer than 2% of respondents are not included in the table.

not in others. One obvious reason for this differential selection of conditions from case to case is that in real-life moral incidents the misdeeds and the features of people and their environments are indeed quite varied. For example, the drastic sanction of death in the cases of the German army officers caused 37 respondents to reject that option because it was incompatible with their value system. They would not condone execution under any circumstance. Since the death penalty was not a suggested option in the remaining cases, this philosophical objection to execution was not a factor influencing respondents' decisions in cases 3 and 4.

In effect, it is a hazardous venture to assume that the conditions respondents apply in one case will be the same as those they apply in another. Understanding the complex system of conditions represented in an individual's moral-reasoning system would appear to require an appraisal of the way that person's multiple considerations are patterned over an array of different types of cases.

In addition to the complexity of people's moral-value structures, another cause of this differential selection of conditions is an artifact of the research method we employed. Our method of collecting people's opinions was basically the same as that used in some of the best-known empirical investigations of moral decision making. A description of a moral incident is presented to respondents who are then asked to explain—either in writing or during an interview—the misdeed or to suggest a solution for the moral dilemma depicted in the anecdote (Kohlberg 1984, pp. 640-651; Piaget, 1932/1948). It is important to recognize how such a situation differs from a person's real-life encounters with moral incidents. In daily life, the people and the components of the environment can be quite complex. Furthermore, events are not frozen but, rather, are in constant motion, confronting observers with a shifting panorama from which they must extract those conditions they believe are important for the moral issue at hand. Which conditions people extract depends on such factors as the perspective from which they view the incident, whether they are active participants or only observers of the event, their emotional state at the time, their acuity of sight and hearing, and more. In contrast, when decisions are derived from brief written descriptions of moral events rather than from true-life encounters, the decision-maker's task is quite different. Moral-incident anecdotes are static, edited versions of real-life episodes. People who constructed the anecdotes have excluded—either on purpose or as an oversight—certain conditions that might affect a particular respondent's judgments, leaving in the description only those conditions that the researchers wished to feature. This matter of edited anecdotes is at least partially responsible for determining which conditions were most frequently cited in the rationales of respondents in the present study. For example, the Nazi colonel's age, state of health, and life-style since World War II were featured in the first case description. In the fourth case, the homeless state of the teenage boy was prominently mentioned. In the third case, the family situation of the drug-peddling girl was conspicuously described. As shown in Table 7-2, these conditions were the ones on which respondents reached the greatest agreement. If the people who participated in our study had actually witnessed in real life the events represented in the written case descriptions, the pattern of conditions they applied when proposing consequences might well have been quite different. Thus, while the results of our opinionnaire survey may accurately reflect some of the conditions respondents considered important when they reasoned about consequences, the picture of conditions revealed by the survey is apparently quite incomplete.

Comparisons of the five respondent groups yielded statistically significant differences for only three of the conditions in Table 7-2—(1) knowledge of right and wrong, (2) inadequate social support, and (3) extent of damage.

In case 5, over 18% percent of San Pablo students censured the man for drinking and driving when he knew it was wrong. However, only 7% of Polk-Metro students—and none from Makai, Pele, or Northcoast—offered such a criticism. Significantly more (.01) San Pablo students (30%) also condemned the medicated woman for likewise being irresponsible.

Substantially more (.001) San Pablo students (37%) than ones from Polk-Metro (16%), Makai (10%), and Pele College (20%) blamed inadequate social support for the plight of the boy who stole the car radio. Lack of social support was also noted by 30% of Northcoast students. San Pablo respondents (29%) referred to social support in the case of the girl who sold drugs, with 18% of the group using insufficient social support as a reason for recommending a less aversive consequence, whereas the remaining 11% said that the girl's unsatisfactory social condition was no reason to excuse her misbehavior. Roughly similar numbers of Pele College (29%) and Northcoast University (22%) students also mentioned the girl's social-support condition, whereas only 2% of Polk-Metro and Makai students did so.

In the incident of the former Nazi colonel, the proportion of respondents who cited the extent of damage as a noteworthy condition was significantly higher (.05) among Northcoast University students (35%) than among ones from Polk-Metro (20%), San Pablo (16%), Makai (16%), or Pele Community College (8%). In the case of the drinking driver, more San Pablo (19%) and Northcoast (16%) respondents mentioned the extent of damage than did students in the other three groups.

To summarize, rarely were there significant differences among the groups in the percentage of students that cited a particular condition. However, in those rare instances there was a greater tendency for San Pablo respondents to cite lack of social support, personal irresponsibility, and extent of damage than was generally true of students from other schools.

Our attempt to achieve a high degree of interrater reliability in identifying conditions was hampered by the fact that the contents of some rationales could logically be listed under more than one type of condition. For example, it would not seem unreasonable to place "He's just a kid, so they shouldn't go too hard on him" under the category *Age Warrants Compassion*, a condition defined as "The transgressor is either too young or too old to deserve strict sanctions." Another example is the comment that "The teenage girl probably lives in a neighborhood where she's under the influence of bad companions, and her mother most likely hasn't given her a good background of values and emotional support." Such a statement might be scored as either of the following conditions:

Inadequate Social Support. The actor did not receive the personal/social support that would encourage law-abiding behavior (inadequate parental guidance, poor models of behavior, lack of reinforcement of good behavior).

Overpowering Personal Problems. The offender's personal problems understandably overwhelmed his or her self-control.

In short, the conditions described in Chapter 3 are not all mutually exclusive. Some overlap, thereby requiring a decision regarding which condition category is the most appropriate in a given case. As noted in the introduction to Part III, the interrater agreement on categorizing conditions averaged 70%. We estimate that the 30% disagreement resulted from a combination of (a) the fact that a process of inference was required for identifying certain of the conditions implied in the individualistic rationales students offered and (b) the overlapping of condition types that would enable one rater to place a rationale under a different condition category than did another rater.

THE ADEQUACY OF OPINIONNAIRE
AND INTERVIEW APPROACHES

In the introduction to Part III we noted that our opinionnaire survey was intended to serve two purposes. The first was to yield information valuable for generating the structure and content of a taxonomy of moral reasoning about consequences people recommend for wrongdoers. The survey appeared to fulfill this aim quite well, for it produced an extended range of principles and conditions. The second purpose was to provide data useful for comparing groups' moral-reasoning patterns. The survey was less successful in achieving this aim because the opinionnaire responses did not provide sufficiently complete information to permit an in-depth analysis of individuals' or groups' modes of thought.

First, under each of the six cases on the opinionnaire, the request to "Tell why you think your choice is the best" was interpreted differently by different respondents. Some answered by simply rewording the consequence they had selected rather than offering reasons for their choice. Such an answer was more often given by high-school students than by those from the community college or university.

Furthermore, among participants who did furnish a rationale to support their consequence, some stated or implied a moral principle but said nothing about conditions of applying the principle nor about the purpose the consequence was expected to serve. Others only stated conditions and wrote nothing about purpose. Still others cited a purpose for a sanction but failed to tell why they believed the sanction would accomplish its intent. In effect, the opinionnaire approach supplied information about no more than a segment of each respondent's way of reasoning rather than producing a comprehensive picture of how people arrived at their decisions. In order to derive a more complete version of people's reasoning patterns, we then created the interview schedule for use with an additional 20 respondents. As noted earlier, the schedule was composed of questions centering on each of the major components of the taxonomy. (See Chapter 10 for a detailed analysis of the interview approach.) As a result of these focused questions, the interview proved far superior to the opinionnaire for eliciting a multifaceted portrayal of participants' thought patterns.

Two more factors that contributed to the opinionnaire's restricted ability to yield a detailed picture of people's reasoning were those of time and of writing space. In filling out the opinionnaire, students were expected to finish six cases within the time of a typical class period. Therefore, they could not dwell long on writing a rationale for any one case. Furthermore, the amount of writing space provided beneath each case was not sufficient to accommodate an extended essay.

An additional shortcoming of the survey, as noted in Chapter 6, was the limited ability of some students to express themselves fluently in written English. Older students who had advanced higher in the formal education system were better equipped to analyze how they thought about the cases and to cast this analysis in writing than were younger respondents who had less schooling.

It is important to recognize that those conditions which respondents cited or implied in their rationales were probably not the only ones affecting their choice of consequences. Hence, any conditions mentioned—or that reasonably could be inferred from a participant's answers—were only those that respondents apparently felt were most necessary for defending the choice of a sanction or else were ones they believed should be brought to the attention of readers. In short, we do not at all assume that rationales offered on the opinionnaires furnished a complete picture of the conditions a given individual included in arriving at the consequence recommendation. The task of learning all the variables influencing such a choice would require a different mode of inquiry. Perhaps the most obvious approach for eliciting a relatively complete pattern of people's conditions would consist of displaying a broad array of possible conditions from which respondents could choose those they regarded as bearing significantly on their selection of consequences in the specific case at hand.

Our reason for identifying the foregoing limitations of the opinionnaire approach has been to alert readers to shortcomings of the group comparisons offered in this chapter and in Chapter 8. The comparisons do not represent the complete thought processes of the members of the several groups. Rather, they reflect only what apparently came uppermost to mind when respondents were asked to "Tell why you think your choice is the best."

CONCLUSION

The results reported in this chapter appear to support the following generalizations about moral principles and about the conditions affecting their application in specific cases of wrongdoing.

1. When people recommend consequences, they seldom explicitly state the moral principles on which they have based their recommendation. Thus, the principles need to be inferred from the type of wrongdoing involved, the suggested consequence, and/or the explanation offered in defense of the consequence.

2. In a group of several dozen or more individuals, the conditions weighed by various group members when they are determining consequences will be

numerous and diverse, with the conditions often differing markedly from one member to another. In other words, there is likely to be relatively little consensus among members about which types of conditions are the most important to consider.

3. In terms of both principles and conditions, the range of diversity within a given group will be greater than the difference between the majority of members of one group and the majority of members of another. This means that knowing the principles and conditions avowed by a particular person is of little or no aid in attempts to estimate from which group that person comes.

4. The principles and conditions that people apply when proposing conse- quences will vary from one case to another, depending on the varied nature of the misdeeds and the individualistic features of the people and their environments in the two cases. Hence, knowing which principles and conditions an individual applies in one case may be of little or no help in predicting the ones he or she will recommend in another case whose characteristics are somewhat different.

The foregoing observations, like those at the close of Chapter 6, call for refinement and revision on the basis of additional empirical studies with other types of cases and other groups of subjects.

8

Purposes, Causes, Feasibility, and Agent Qualifications

After analyzing respondents' moral values in Chapter 7, we turn now to the remaining four components of the taxonomy—the purposes of consequences, causes related to misdeeds and sanctions, the feasibility of consequences, and agents considered qualified to propose consequences.

THE PURPOSES OF CONSEQUENCES

Purposes that respondents intended their consequences to serve were inferred from opinionnaire replies in two ways:

1. From the nature of the consequence itself.
    "The woman should pay the medical bills of the boy she injured."
       (Scored as *Compensate the Victim.*)
    "They could require the major to do community service and therefore make up a
       bit for all the suffering he caused."
       (Scored as *Compensate Society.*)
2. From the rationale offered in defense of the consequence.
    "If he has to spend time in jail, maybe he'll learn to be a responsible driver."
       (Scored as *Teach Accountability.*)
    "Putting the boy in a good foster home could help him straighten out his life."
       (Scored as *Reform the Offender.*)

The type of answer that respondents offered in their rationales did not always lend itself to deriving an apparent consequence. Therefore, the results reported in this section are based on approximately 65% of the cases of wrongdoing that the 416 students addressed.

In our original process of inspecting the 416 opinionnaires from the five U.S. groups, we derived the 26 purposes described in Chapter 4. It was apparent that many of the 26 were not mutually exclusive but, rather, could be interrelated in several ways. We then faced the choice of merely listing the 26 or of placing them in categories that might reflect something of the relationships among them. As explained in Chapter 4, we adopted the second option by dividing the types of purposes among three sets labeled *Intended Ultimate Results, Instrumental Aims,* and *Implementing Aims.* We considered instrumental aims to be ones that contributed to the achievement of ultimate results, and we conceived implementing aims to be ones that promoted both instrumental goals and ultimate results. Although there was some virtue in this scheme, in practice it proved to be marred by two shortcomings.

First, with only the brief opinionnaire answers in hand, we did not know whether a respondent intended an inferred purpose to be an ultimate result rather than an instrumental or implementing aim. For instance, how should we score such a recommendation as "The Nazi major deserves to be killed for what he did"? Is this the implementing aim of *Harming the Offender* or the ultimate result of *Matching the Act*? Or perhaps the respondent considered harming the offender to be not just an implementing step but the ultimate purpose of the sanction—harming the transgressor solely for the sake of inflicting pain, with no other end in mind.

Second, respondents may have intended their proposed consequence to accomplish not just one aim but a variety, with only one or two of them reflected in the brief rationale written in defense of the proposal. To illustrate, we judged that the following statement should be scored as both the implementing aim of *Generating Affect* and the ultimate result of *Controlling the Offender's Behavior*: "Let him see how it feels to be locked up where he can't be out drinking and driving." But in addition, it seems likely that a person might hope such a sanction would also *Wreak Revenge, Teach Accountability, Implement the Law,* and *Deter Others.* However, the opinionnaire format, with its question that simply asked why the respondent offered a particular consequence, was not well suited to completely plumbing the individual's entire array of purposes. The 20 interviews, which included a question aimed specifically at purposes, proved more adequate. An even better method would have been to ask interviewees for the intended goal of their proposal, then to furnish them a list of possible purposes (such as the 26 in Chapter 4) and ask them to identify any others in the list that they hoped their consequence might accomplish. However, adopting such a detailed procedure would greatly lengthen interview time and thereby markedly reduce the number of participants who could feasibly be included in the survey.

The difficulties posed by the foregoing limitations reduced the interrater reliability of the scoring of purposes to around 84%. If, in preparing the scoring sheets, we had included a grater array of sample responses under each of the 26 categories, the reliability might have been increased; but the idiosyncratic nature of students' written rationales renders it unlikely that interrater agreement would ever approach 100%.

In summary, the opinionnaire approach enabled us to elicit the ideas of a large number of respondents, but it did not permit an in-depth analysis of the range of purposes that individuals wanted their consequences to achieve. Therefore, the opinionnaire survey was more successful in producing a wide selection of purposes to include in the taxonomy than it was in revealing the scope of purposes that each individual had in mind.

Table 8-1 displays the percentages of each purpose in each of the six cases as inferred from the 416 opinionnaires. The meaning attached to the percentages should be qualified by the caveats described above. That is, the percentages only reflect the purposes that might be inferred from 65% of the cases to which survey participants responded. Those purposes were limited to ones that apparently came prominently to mind as students offered consequences and supporting rationales. In the 20 interviews that followed the opinionnaire

Table 8-1

Purposes Implied in the Six Cases
(in percentages, N = 416)

Type of Purpose	*The Cases*					
	Army Colonel	*Army Major*	*Girl & Drugs*	*Boy & Stereo*	*Drinking Driver*	*Medicated Driver*
—Intended Ultimate Result—						
Implement the Law	19	20	11	6	11	7
Compensate the Victim	1			1	50	48
Teach Accountability	3	2	9	6	13	13
Protect Society	2	3	2	1		
Teach Right & Wrong			6	4	6	4
Teach to Respect Authority				1		
Acknowledge Damage	6	7	4	2	6	6
Match the Misdeed	7	4				
Match the Deed's Severity		1	1		1	
Wreak Revenge	1	2				
Protect Individual's Rights		1				
Compensate Society	2		1		2	1
—Instrumental Aims—						
Reform the Offender	1		27	34	6	2
Prevent Future Misdeeds	2	4	6	6	6	4
Deter Others	2	2	2	1	3	1
—Implementing Aims—						
Harm the Offender	6	7		1	1	
Self-Improvement Chance			8	10		
Alter Offender's Skills/Values			3	6	2	
Remove Chance of Misdeed				1		
Remove Improper Influences			3	3		
Generate Affect		1		2	1	1
Reform Offender's Caretakers				2		

Note: Four purposes mentioned by less than 1% of respondents are not included in the table. They are: *Teach Respect for the Law, Save Money, Reduce Victim's Anger,* and *Monitor Victim's Behavior.*

survey, when respondents were asked the purpose of their consequences, all could readily offer an answer. Such a result suggests that all, or nearly all, of the opinionnaire respondents could have stated what they intended their sanctions to accomplish if they had been specifically asked. Therefore, the results reported in Table 8-1 provide only a partial picture of the purposes behind the consequences recommended by the 416 subjects in the opinionnaire survey.

The percentages in Table 8-1 show that the popularity of purposes sometimes varied from one type of case to another. In the incident of the two army officers, the desire of one-fifth of the respondents was to ensure that the law governing wartime crimes was enforced. The two principal aims for both of the reckless motorists were to compensate their accident victims and to hold the motorists accountable for their irresponsible behavior. The most popular purpose for the pair of delinquent teenagers was to effect a reformation in their life-styles. On the other hand, the incidence of certain purposes was essentially the same across most or all types of cases. Such was true for the aims of *Acknowledging the Damage, Preventing Misdeeds,* and *Deterring Others from Wrongdoing.*

A comparison among the five American groups revealed that in only four types of purposes were there differences between one group and another that reached statistically significant levels. In the two cases of former German army officers, from 14% to 17% of San Pablo Parochial High students proposed consequences that would acknowledge the damage done, whereas no students from the other four schools implied such a purpose. In the case of the army major, significantly more (.01) Polk-Metro (29%) than San Pablo (14%) respondents hoped to guarantee that the law was implemented. The intent to reform the girl who had stabbed the teacher was expressed by a significantly larger (.001) proportion of Northcoast University students (46%) than by students from any of the three high schools (Polk Metro 20%, Makai 23%, San Pablo 25%). The percentage of Pele Community College students (33%) proposing reform fell midway between the Northcoast and the high-school figures. In the incident of the stolen car radio, significantly more (.001) respondents from Northcoast (49%), San Pablo (42%), and Pele (38%) aimed at reforming the boy than did respondents from Polk-Metro (19%) and Makai (23%) high schools.

These comparisons hint at something about attitudes that perhaps typify the five groups of students. As noted in Chapters 6 and 7, Polk-Metro and Makai High School students were alike in several ways that differentiated them from Pele College and Northcoast University students and, to a lesser extent, from the San Pablo Parochial High group. The socioeconomic status of Polk-Metro and Makai respondents was less favorable than that of the other three groups. There was also a higher incidence of crime in the Polk-Metro and Makai communities. The written communication skills of Polk-Metro and Makai students were inferior to those of San Pablo, Pele, and Northcoast participants. Furthermore, Polk-Metro and Makai respondents displayed considerably less initiative in suggesting alternative consequences to those listed below the cases. In effect, the groups could be divided into two general categories differentiated by socioeconomic status, the incidence of crime in the community, respondents' observations of the typical treatment of wrongdoing in their neighborhoods, level of academic achievement, and initiative in generating consequences and rationales. This combination of factors may have led Polk-Metro and Makai students to place somewhat greater emphasis on implementing the law by applying traditional punishments. In contrast, Northcoast, Pele, and San Pablo students seemed more prone to devise consequences that represented positive efforts to reform wrongdoers.

CAUSALITY

As explained in Chapter 4, respondents could relate causality to consequences in two ways. As the first possibility, they could estimate what caused the offender to do wrong, and then the consequence they proposed would be intended to correct such a cause. For instance, if the estimated reason behind the teenage boy's stealing a car radio was that his parents had employed unsuitable child-rearing techniques when the boy was growing up, then the best remedy might be to place him in a foster home where constructive child-raising methods were practiced. As the second option, respondents could reflect their convictions about causality by explaining why they believed their proposed consequence would achieve its purposes. To illustrate, they could contend that a jail term would be so painful for the drinking driver that he would endeavor to mend his driving habits in order to avoid a similar punishment in the future.

Our analysis of opinionnaire answers showed that few subjects directly described the way they perceived causation operating in the cases. This paucity of direct statements about cause was not likely a result of the respondents' failing to ground their proposed consequences on a concept of causality. In the interview portion of our investigation, all 20 participants readily produced cause rationales when they were specifically asked to do so. Hence, the shortage of cause statements in the opinionnaire survey apparently occurred because most respondents perceived such factors as moral conditions and purposes as being the most suitable matters to mention in defending their consequence recommendations.

Because direct estimates of cause were rare in the rationales, we were obliged to infer students' concepts of cause either from the nature of a recommended consequence or from some aspect of a supporting rationale.

In Chapter 4 we identified four ways to view issues of causation in relation to people's proposals of consequences. Causality could be conceived in terms of (1) underlying versus immediate factors, (2) heredity interacting with environmental forces, (3) a process by which environmental factors could effect changes in people's behavior, and (4) the motives behind people's actions. In the following paragraphs we describe results of the opinionnaire survey from these four perspectives.

Underlying Versus Immediate Factors

Underlying factors, as defined in Chapter 4, are conditions that derive from a person's past and that persist into the present. Proximate, precipitating, or immediate factors are influences of very recent origin. The most noteworthy factors that fit these two categories in our present study are shown in Table 8-2.

The figures within the table represent the percentage of respondents who cited each of the factors as a contributor to misdeeds in the six cases. Underlying factors were obviously proposed far more often than immediate ones.

The types of character traits or personality features that were judged to be faulty varied somewhat according to the type of wrongdoing under consideration. The army officers were depicted as vicious and mean-spirited. The teenagers were censured for being malicious and out of control. The two motorists were denounced for stupidity and bad judgment.

The families of the two teenagers were criticized for not providing appropriate social support. In particular, the homeless boy's parents were accused by more than one-quarter of the respondents with failing to display the understanding, patience, care, and firm guidance that adolescents require. When respondents alluded to a difficult home situation without directly placing blame on the two teenagers' caretakers, the cause was listed under *Family Situation*. In the case of the drinking driver, the man's divorce was the event viewed as the undesirable family situation behind his auto accident. A small number of respondents denounced society in general for failing to furnish the support and opportunities young people need to grow up as moral citizens.

The obligations that the former Nazis incurred as military officers were cited by around 5% of respondents as causes for the deaths of the partisans.

In the cases of the motorists, the two immediate factors cited by participants were those of alcohol and drugs. A small proportion of respondents proposed surprise and shock as factors causing the girl to stab the teacher and the boy to hit the officer when the two youths were suddenly apprehended in criminal acts.

Table 8-2

Underlying and Immediate Causes
(in percentages, N = 416)

Type of Cause	The Cases					
	Army Colonel	Army Major	Girl & Drugs	Boy & Stereo	Drinking Driver	Medicated Driver
—Underlying Factors—						
Faulty Character Traits	3	2	1	3	3	17
Inadequate Social Support			19	26		
Family Situation			9	4	10	
Role Obligations	5	6				
Society in General			1	1		
—Immediate Factors—						
Drinking Alcohol					2	
Using a Drug						2
Sudden Apprehension			2	4		

Comparisons among the five groups of respondents revealed no significant differences between one group and another in regard to underlying and proximate causes.

Heredity-Environment Interactions

Whereas respondents referred to a host of environmental forces as determinants in wrongdoing, none directly referred to heredity as a contributing factor. The single factor which some respondents may have believed derived from offenders' genetic endowment was that of faulty character traits. In Chapter 4 we noted that some moral-behavior theorists have proposed that certain personality features —honesty, aggressivity, viciousness, social sensitivity, and others—are at least partially innate. Other theorists disagree; they contend that such personality characteristics are not inborn but, rather, are learned during a person's formative years. Although some of our respondents blamed faulty character traits for offenders' misdeeds, we do not know the extent to which participants thought such traits were a result of heredity rather than environmental influences. In any event, among those respondents who included cause estimates in their rationales, the overwhelming majority cited environmental factors as the reasons behind the wrongdoing. The frequency of such cause attributions is shown in Table 8-3.

Implementing any of the consequences recommended by survey participants would necessarily require action on the part of specified individuals or agencies. These providers of consequences—as the executors of sanctions and treatments— become the responsible causal agents. The types of responsible agents implied in the consequences offered by the 416 American students are summarized in Table 8-4. Personnel in judicial and penal systems would be the agents responsible for imposing consequences recommended by all participants in the cases of the army officers and the motorists. However, a variety of other kinds of people would be involved in administering those consequences recommended

Table 8-3

Heredity & Environment Sources of Misdeeds
(in percentages, N = 416)

Type of Source	*Army Colonel*	*Army Major*	*Girl & Drugs*	*Boy & Stereo*	*Drinking Driver*	*Medicated Driver*
	The Cases					
	—Hereditary Factors—					
None Specified						
	—Environmental Factors—					
Inadequate Social Support			19	26		
Family/Parents			9	4	10	
Role Obligations	5	6				
Drugs/Alcohol					2	2
The Social System	1	1	1	1		

Table 8-4

Providers of Consequences
(in percentages, N = 416)

	The Cases					
Type of *Source*	*Army* *Colonel*	*Army* *Major*	*Girl &* *Drugs*	*Boy &* *Stereo*	*Drinking* *Driver*	*Medicated* *Driver*
Judiciary/Penal System	100	100	67	43	100	100
Probation Personnel			13	55		
School Personnel			8	60		
Counselors/Therapists			8	11	4	
Foster Caretakers			3	61		

for the pair of delinquent juveniles. In none of the cases were family members assigned responsibility for carrying out consequences.

A Process of Environmental Influence

In Chapter 4 we suggested four aspects of a process through which environmental factors might alter an individual's moral reasoning and behavior. The aspects were (1) the kinds of moral events an individual experiences, (2) the values reflected in other people's responses to those events, (3) the models that an individual chooses to imitate, and (4) the kinds of consequences the individuals experienced in the past. We inspected the 416 completed opinionnaires to learn how many participants mentioned any of these aspects when accounting either (a) for the offender's misdeed or (b) for why a proposed consequence would likely achieve its purpose. The analysis revealed that in hardly a dozen instances did respondents refer specifically to any of the four aspects of the process. A few suggested that the German army major had witnessed the consequences others had suffered for disobeying orders, so that he supervised the executions in order to avoid a similar fate. Several proposed that the homeless teenage boy had been influenced by undesirable peer models. However, most respondents alluded only generally to a process of environmental influence. For instance, in the case of the teenage boy, 26% of the 416 participants blamed his parents for deficient child-rearing practices; 17% blamed general family conditions for the teenage girl's drug-peddling activities.

In a similar way, most respondents' reasons for why their proposed consequences could prevent future wrongdoing were unspecific, expressed in such imprecise phrases as "a good foster-home situation" or "proper counseling." The characteristics that would represent a good home or proper counseling were not described.

In an effort to account for such results, we surmised that a variety of factors conspired against the likelihood that respondents would analyze the process of environmental influence in any detail. First, the opinionnaire format did not lend itself to lengthy explanations, particularly because most of the students were working within the time constraint of one class period. Furthermore, respondents were not asked specifically to offer cause estimates. They were simply asked to tell why their consequence was appropriate; most chose to write about some aspect of the cases other than matters of cause. In addition, the case descriptions were very brief, offering little guidance to respondents regarding a multiplicity of further conditions that might have contributed to the wrongdoing.

Thus, while respondents' conceptions of causation are undoubtedly important for understanding their patterns of moral reasoning, our opinionnaire format was not well suited to delineating those patterns. The interviews were more productive, since they included specific questions about cause.

Motives as Causes

In fewer than 2% of the cases judged by the 416 American participants were misdeeds attributed to offenders' intentions. Because the citations of motives were so few, in Table 8-5 we have reported them as numbers of instances rather than as percentages.

The most frequent mention of motives occurred in the cases of the two adolescents. Sixteen respondents surmised that the girl sold drugs to get money to help support her family. Five estimated that the reason the boy stole the radio was so he might sell it and have money to survive on the streets. Two participants speculated that the woman motorist disobeyed the physician's warning because she needed to buy food. Feelings of anger and frustration at their life conditions were cited as motives for the girl's selling drugs and stabbing the teacher, for the boy's stealing and striking the police officer, and for the divorced motorist's drinking and driving. In three instances, the army officers' fear that they would be disciplined for failing to carry out their duty was blamed for their killing the partisans. One respondent judged that the 13-year-old boy hit the policeman because the boy was afraid of being arrested. Three wrote

Table 8-5

Estimates of Offenders' Motives
(in numbers of instances, N = 416)

	The Cases					
Type of Motive	*Army Colonel*	*Army Major*	*Girl & Drugs*	*Boy & Stereo*	*Drinking Driver*	*Medicated Driver*
Obtain Items for Survival			16	5		2
Anger, Frustration			3	14	2	
Self Defense, Fear	1	2		1		
Desire to Be Helpful	3					
Revenge				1		
Malice, Hate	1					

that the army colonel was motivated by the conviction that he was doing something good for the world when he executed enemies, whereas one respondent blamed the executions on the colonel's malicious nature. Finally, one participant in the survey estimated that the teenage boy's delinquent acts were committed as revenge against his parents.

Although there were no statistically significant differences among the five groups of American students, there was a noticeable tendency for more San Pablo respondents to cite anger and frustration as the cause of the teenage boy's misdeeds than was true of members of the other groups. What this tendency might signify about the nature of the San Pablo sample is not apparent.

In summary, when participants sought to explain why they recommended a particular consequence, only a few cited offenders' motives as the reason for misconduct. A far greater number alluded to environmental forces as the causes behind wrongdoing. Most of the proposed motives were of two general varieties —ones involving attempts to obtain items that would fulfill the transgressors' desires and others involving the expression of such negative emotions as anger, fear, and hate.

Individual Patterns of Cause Attribution

Among the questions asked during the 20 interviews, two focused on causation: (1) What caused the offender to do wrong? (2) Why do you believe your consequence would work? Respondents' replies revealed a diversity of ways that people may conceive of cause. That diversity is reflected in the following four excerpts from the 20 interviews. In each example, the first answer is to the question of why the offender committed the misdeed. Four ways in which respondents' answers could differ from each other were in who they identified as the causal agent, in the general nature of the cause, in the variety of causal options included, and in the specificity of the description of cause. These four aspects are defined as follows:

Causal Agent: Who or what deserves the blame for the misdeed?
General Nature of the Cause: What label identifies the type of cause?
Variety of Causal Options: How many likely causes are considered?
Specificity of Cause Description: How detailed is the explanation of the estimated cause of the wrongdoing?

The second segment of each example answers the question of why respondents believed their proposed consequences would succeed. Four ways that this portion could differ from one respondent to another are in who they identified as the responsible agent, in the general nature of the consequence, in the relationship of the consequence to the cause of the misdeed, and in the specificity of the consequence description. These variables are defined as:

Responsible Agent: Who bears the responsibility to implement the sanction or treatment?
General Nature of the Consequence: What label identifies the type of sanction or treatment?
Cause/Consequence Relationship: Is the consequence intended to correct the original cause or not?

Specificity of Consequence Description: How detailed is the explanation of why the consequence should achieve its aim?

Respondent W—a 45-year-old male In the case of the boy who stole the car radio, Respondent W contends that the causal agent was not the boy but, rather, his parents. This cause could be labeled "improper child-rearing practices." The respondent does not describe those practices in detail. The recommended treatment (foster home, school, probation) is intended to remedy the improper child rearing. The responsible agents are foster parents, teachers, and probation personnel. The intended treatment is described in only moderately specific terms.

> (Why did the boy steal the stereo?) "He's a product of society—of the way he's been socialized. The parents weren't qualified. They weren't capable. They didn't treat him right."
>
> (Why would the recommended consequence succeed?) "A 13-year-old child needs the cohesion that comes with a home atmosphere, so the foster home could provide that. We're talking here about self-esteem, and to get that you have to have a supportive family. He also needs a good school situation. A good probation officer can see that both a good foster home and a good school setting will be provided. The boy needs a lot of love, a lot of care, a lot of attention. He needs a supportive atmosphere that is secure, has continuity, and has permanence; and the only place to get that is in a loving home. That type of treatment could turn a 13-year-old boy around."

Respondent X—a 37-year-old male In his reaction to Case 5, Respondent X cites the driver and his drinking as the causal agents and posits two causes that could be labeled "emotional distress" and "intoxication." Furthermore, he rationalizes the causes in some detail. Part of the consequence (paying medical costs) is not intended to cure the cause but, instead, it is to see that some justice is provided for the victims of the accident. The other part of the consequence (a fine and a jail term) is intended to remedy an estimated cause, that is, to correct the errant motorist's drink-and-drive behavior.

> (What caused the accident?) "I'm assuming the drinking and/or anger—that is, having his mind preoccupied and the effect of the alcohol. The description doesn't say that he drank because of the divorce. Myself, I'd have been angry after drinking, so it's hard for me to say that the reason he drank was because he was angry about his wife divorcing him. That's a possibility, but I don't really know. But the alcohol, I think, really caused the accident."
>
> (Why would the recommended consequence succeed?) "I think that paying the medical costs of the injured women is justice; that benefits the women. But the rest—the $1,000 fine and weekends in jail—that sends this guy a message that may help rehabilitate him. If he's got a lot of money, writing a check for $1,000 isn't such a big thing. But the jail time, that would make an impression. It should make him think pretty hard about what he's done."

Respondent Y—a 9-year-old female In her critique of the teenage girl's drug selling, Respondent Y suggests a single cause, which could be labeled *peer influence.* The causal agents are identified as the offender's companions who take advantage of the offender's susceptibility to their influence. The way such influence has operated is not explained in detail. The sanction of sending the girl to a detention facility could be labeled *incarceration*, with juvenile-hall personnel responsible for administering the consequence. Respondent Y implies that being confined for a year would deter the girl from committing such misdeeds in the future. No details are offered about what sorts of experiences at the juvenile center would be needed to teach the girl the desired lesson.

> (What caused her to sell drugs?) "Maybe her friends were saying she should do it, and she didn't want to put them down by not doing what they said."
> (Why would the recommended consequence succeed?) "If she were to go to juvenile hall for a year, then maybe it would teach her a lesson about what she did and make her think twice about doing it the next time."

Respondent Z—a 12-year-old male In his reaction to the case of the former army colonel, Respondent Z blames the colonel as the causal agent, citing two interlinked causes that might be labeled *faulty character traits*. The way such traits developed or why they arose in the Yugoslav situation is not specified. Respondent Z proposes that the colonel be executed, with the Yugoslav judicial system apparently the agent responsible for carrying out that sanction. No details are offered about how the execution should be performed. The respondent does not specify the purpose of the sanction—whether it is to wreak revenge, implement the law, prevent future misdeeds, or what? Therefore, rather than explaining why the recommended sanction would achieve its purpose, he suggests that executing the wrongdoer would somehow benefit both the offender and the Yugoslav population.

> (What caused the misdeed?) "Maybe he was just a vicious man, and maybe he hated the Yugoslavians anyway, so he just killed them."
> (Why would the recommended consequence succeed?) "The jury found him guilty, so he should be killed. He already has a kidney failure, so if he was allowed to return home it would be just as bad a punishment. And if he stayed in the prison, he was just going to die anyway. So just kill him now. It's almost like it's good for him and good for the Yugoslavians, too."

CONSEQUENCE FEASIBILITY

Evidence that respondents were concerned about the feasibility of consequences appeared in rationales that explained why one potential consequence was preferable to another. The instances in which respondents offered this sort of comparison were quite rare, as indicated in Table 8-6 where the occurrence of various kinds of feasibility is displayed. In contrast to the figures that have appeared in most other tables, those in Table 8-6 represent numbers of instances rather than the percentage of respondents who alluded to a given feasibility characteristic. Frequencies rather than percentages were used here because so few instances of feasibility considerations appeared. In way of illustration, the number 7 in the second row for the case of the drug-peddling teenage girl means that 7 of the 416 American participants in the opinionnaire survey mentioned unwanted side effects that might accompany a potential sanction. The following are typical rationales that qualified for the bad-side-effects category in case 3:

> "If the girl is allowed to remain at home, she'll just continue to be a bad influence on her sisters, so she'd better go to the juvenile center."

Table 8-6

Feasibility   Considerations in the Six Cases
(in numbers of instances, N=416)

Type of Feasibility	Army Colonel	Army Major	Girl & Drugs	Boy & Stereo	Drinking Driver	Medicated Driver
			The Cases			
Effectiveness	13	5	13	3	2	7
Unwanted Side Effects	7	1	7	4	4	9
Financial Expense	10	5	3		5	
Inconvenience	2	2				
Facility Availability	1		1			1

"The girl may have been selling drugs to get money for her family. Sending her to a detention facility for a year would keep her from helping support the family. It would be better to keep her at home and see that she gets a legitimate job."

"If there is a chance that she can recover some self-esteem, throwing her in juvenile hall might take away any self-esteem that she has left, so she might just give up and say, 'See, they're right. I'm really bad.' Rather than juvenile hall, she needs extensive counseling."

As these comments suggest, each of the feasibility considerations displayed in Table 8-6 appeared in a comparative context. A respondent would contend that consequence Y, as compared with consequence Z, was less desirable because Y was less practical. The greatest number of such comparisons were offered in the cases of the army colonel and the girl who sold drugs, apparently because more respondents felt that their recommended consequences in those cases would not appear reasonable unless defended on the grounds of practicality. We estimate that many more feasibility reasons would be offered by respondents if they were asked to compare the advantages and disadvantages of all the consequence options under a given case. In effect, we believe that the rare mention of feasibility factors in opinionnaire rationales was due more to the students' attention focusing on other aspects of the taxonomy rather than to any lack of opinions about which consequences were more practical than others. Evidence from the 20 interviews supports this impression. When interviewees were specifically asked why they preferred their consequence choice over the remaining options, all of them readily came up with reasons, some of which related to feasibility.

Comparisons of the five American groups revealed no significant differences in the number or types of feasibility factors included in the groups' rationales.

QUALIFIED AGENTS

The idea that agent qualifications should be included as a taxonomy category occurred to us when 5 of the 542 participants in the opinionnaire survey declined to offer a consequence for one or more cases on the grounds that they were not qualified to do so. In 4 of these 5 instances, the objection to recommending a sanction was voiced in the cases of the two German army officers who, according to the listed consequence options, faced possible death or life imprisonment. The 4 respondents excused themselves from this task by offering such reasons as, "It's God's right, not mine" or "A higher power decides these things." A fifth student avoided deciding the fate to be faced by the teenage drug peddler by writing, "I don't know enough about the details of the case to offer a proper opinion."

As a means of investigating the matter of agent qualifications more fully, we included the following question in the 20 interviews that were conducted after completing the opinionnaire survey:

> You've been willing to suggest consequences in this case. But some people aren't willing. They say it's not their right to propose consequences. Do you think everybody has that right? That is, who does and who doesn't have the right, and why?

The first two interviews revealed that participants saw the matter of agent qualifications as involving two questions rather than just one. The first question was: "Who has the right to <u>offer an opinion</u> about what consequences might be proper in cases of wrongdoing?" The second was: "Who <u>bears the responsibility</u> for imposing the consequences that an offender will actually experience?" In recognition of the dual meaning that our original question could imply, in all subsequent interviews both of these questions were asked.

Question 1: Who has the right to offer an opinion? All 20 participants said that everyone has that right. This conviction was buttressed with such reasons as the following:

> "Just like I have my own opinion, someone else can have their own opinion, too. And both could be heard."
> "Sure. Proposing consequences is not making decisions or handing down edicts. To me, proposing consequences is a way of contributing to a situation that needs to be alleviated. So, if your knowledge can help solve the problem, what else is knowledge for?"
> "I have the right as much as anybody else."
> "If someone has done something to hurt society or the good of all and has disobeyed laws that are set by the majority, then we have the right to decide the consequences. That's what this country is built on. We all have that right."
> "Whenever the wrongdoing is something that affects society, then I think we all have a responsibility to say that behavior isn't appropriate and can't continue. So in that way we all are responsible for suggesting consequences."

Question 2: Who bears responsibility for actually imposing consequences? Answers to this query varied somewhat from one respondent to another and from one case of wrongdoing to another. The examples below illustrate typical agents that were considered properly qualified in different cases.

> "For the German colonel, it's up to whoever's in charge, like the Yugoslavian government."

"In the case of the Nazi major, maybe the families of the dead Yugoslavs could do it. There's an interesting idea."

"I guess a jury. Choose 12 people and they decide. That's the system we have, whether it's good or not."

"The judicial system—the police, the jury, the judge."

"For the boy who stole the radio, his parents should be involved, along with a judge for juveniles; and the boy should have a say in it, too. He's 13 years old. That's old enough to realize he's done something wrong."

"When kids do wrong? Well, the parents—and police officers."

Some interviewees, who readily proposed consequences and contended that anyone has a right to do so, were nevertheless unwilling in real-life situations to assume a direct role in imposing sanctions. One reason was that they felt technically unqualified for such responsibility.

A 36-year-old man "I think everybody has the right to an opinion about consequences. But it's tricky business. With the knowledge I have at this time in my life, I certainly wouldn't want to propose consequences that would be written into laws that affect other people's lives. If I wanted to make that my career or my life's quest, I would make sure I had as much training as I could in the law, and then I'd try to make the best judgments I could. It's an awesome responsibility to be passing and exercising laws that influence others' lives. The only way we can make an organized society work is to choose certain people to hold the authority to impose consequences, such as to hold positions in the court system. The right to pass and impose consequences should be held by only those that we in a participatory democracy decide should have that right—we elect them as our representatives."

A 42-year-old man "I have as much right as anybody else to say what I think should be done. But should consequences be carried out on my say-so? No, I don't think I'm a jury of one with the right to say for this particular person what should automatically happen. I would like to hear some other people's ideas to maybe rebut my opinion. So I think it should be done by a committee."

The reason other respondents would avoid establishing consequences in real-life cases was not that they felt technically unfit but, rather, they considered the responsibility too great an emotional burden. For instance, a 40-year-old woman did not hesitate to recommend death for the Nazi major who supervised the execution of Yugoslavs. However, when asked who actually would be qualified to impose such a sentence, she said:

"Anybody has the right to feel this way or that way. I have a right to say what I think should happen. But who has the right to make the final decision? I certainly wouldn't want to be that person. I couldn't myself see that someone was killed."

A third set of interviewees would not like to determine the sanctions to be imposed in actual life situations because they contended that agencies already existed to fill such a role. As one respondent remarked, "It's not my job, not my responsibility." Such was their position even when they were not entirely satisfied with the performance of those agencies.

"You like to think that people operating the judicial system are doing the best they can, but I hate to put my faith in the system after seeing how some trials come out."

In summary, all 20 interview subjects believed that everybody has the right to express an opinion about consequences for wrongdoers, but no one believed that everybody has the right or responsibility to impose the consequences that offenders will in fact experience.

The interview results were used to aid us in speculating about the beliefs likely held by the opinionnaire respondents. We may recall that only 5 of the 542 who completed questionnaires considered themselves unqualified even to offer an opinion about suitable sanctions in at least some cases. The remaining 537 did indeed propose what should happen to transgressors. Thus, we assume that these 537, like the 20 interviewees, believed that anybody has a right to express an opinion. On the other hand, from our experience with the 20 interviewees, we would guess that few, if any, of the 537 would think that everybody has the right and responsibility to determine consequences wrongdoers will actually experience. Instead, we believe that most or all respondents would cite particular agents as the ones qualified to offer such final judgments.

CONCLUSION

In Chapter 8 we have reported the way four components of the taxonomy of moral-reasoning (purposes, causes, feasibility conditions, agent qualifications) were reflected in the opinionnaire responses of the 416 members of the five American groups that participated in this study. Respondents were not asked specifically to address those components. Rather, they were asked only to explain why the consequences they recommended were appropriate. Thus, the results offered in this chapter are based on only the answers of the people who happened to include one or more of the components in their explanations. The report of opinionnaire results has been supplemented with excerpts from the 20 interviews that were conducted after the opinionnaire survey was completed.

Among the 26 purposes of consequences extracted from the 416 opinionnaires, the 6 that were most frequently implied in respondents' answers were those of (1) ensuring that laws are implemented, (2) compensating victims of wrongdoing, (3) reforming the wrongdoers, (4) holding them accountable for their actions, (5) acknowledging the damage done, and (6) preventing similar misdeeds in the future.

Causes of the transgressions in the cases, as inferred from opinionnaire responses, were viewed from four perspectives: (1) underlying versus proximate factors, (2) heredity-environment interactions, (2) a process of environmental influence, and (4) offenders' motives.

The analysis of opinionnaires showed that underlying factors were mentioned far more often than immediate factors in accounting for offenders' misdeeds. The underlying causes most often mentioned were offenders' undesirable personality traits, the inadequate social support and guidance they received (particularly from family members), and obligations the offenders incurred because of their occupational roles. Heredity was rarely, if ever, suggested as a cause of wrongdoing. Instead, a variety of environmental variables were blamed. When addressing the question of how environmental forces could effect offenders' behavior, respondents rarely specified steps that the process would involve. Instead, their allusions to the process were cast in imprecise phrases, such as "The boy needed better parents" or "He didn't have love and understanding" or "They didn't give him proper discipline." In fewer than 2% of the cases, respondents cited offenders' motives as causes of wrongdoing. Those motives included the desire to obtain objects (money, food) for personal survival, to vent anger and frustration, to defend oneself, and to do the right thing (such as fulfilling one's obligations).

Some respondents rejected certain consequence options on the grounds of feasibility. Feasibility considerations included those of consequence effectiveness, undesirable side effects, cost, inconvenience, and the availability of suitable facilities.

Finally, in a few cases respondents declined to recommend a consequence, since they felt they lacked the right and the qualifications to make such a decision. In order to investigate this issue in greater detail, we included in the 20 interviews a pair of questions focusing specifically on the matter of agent qualifications. The results showed that all interviewees believed they had the right to express an opinion about which consequences seemed most appropriate, but they thought that the responsibility of determining which consequences would actually be imposed rested in the hands of designated individuals, such as the police, court officials, members of juries, probation officers, and parents.

9

Gender Comparisons

For more than a decade an emotionally charged debate in the professional literature has focused on the question of whether women base their moral judgments on different principles than those used by men. The debate has centered around a conflict of opinion between two Harvard University professors. Lawrence Kohlberg (1984) proposed that mature moral judgments were founded on (a) people reaching an agreement about rules of justice and (b) the even-handed application of those rules to all members of the society. Carol Gilligan contended that Kohlberg's observation might account for some people's behavior —such as typical male judgments—but it failed to account for the moral decisions of others—particularly of mature women. For these others, Gilligan held that compassionate caring, as associated with traditional female social roles and the act of mothering, was the guide to moral decision-making (Gilligan, 1982; Gilligan, Ward, & Taylor, 1988).

As we prepared the six cases for the present study, we thought the data we would gather might be useful in appraising the positions of Kohlberg and Gilligan. Therefore, in constructing the cases we included some consequence choices that appeared indicative of Kohlberg's position and others that seemed closer to Gilligan's perspective. In effect, in the consequence choices listed under each of the six cases of wrongdoing, the earliest choice is intended to be closer to Kohlberg's evenhanded-justice perspective and the last choice (prior to the option labeled "other") closer to Gilligan's compassionate caring.

In order to estimate whether the choices under the six cases did, indeed, reflect such contrasting conceptions, we needed a definition of each position. Our review of the works of Kohlberg and Gilligan failed to yield the brief, clear-cut definitions we desired, so we constructed the following pair, hoping they would approximate what Kohlberg and Gilligan intended:

Evenhanded Justice: The highest good lies in applying moral rules (laws) equally to all people who are intellectually mature enough both to understand the rules and to recognize the consequences of abiding by or transgressing them.

Compassionate Caring: The highest good lies in sympathizing with and caring for the welfare of people in need. Those who transgress the law by interfering with others' rights or privileges should be forgiven their transgressions, protected from retribution, and given a chance to make a fresh start.

To determine the extent to which judges not associated with the present study would agree with our assumption about which consequences in the six cases were associated with which of the two contrasting viewpoints, we asked 34 graduate students in the fields of educational psychology and teacher education to rank the options in each of the six cases from (a) the choice that most closely represented the definition of evenhanded justice to (b) the choice that most nearly reflected the definition of compassionate caring. For the purpose of this exercise, the consequence options were listed in random order, rather than in the sequence in which they appeared on the opinionnaire described in Chapter 2.

The judges, each working independently, agreed with the researchers' intention for the first and last choices (with the "other" choice omitted) in 92% of the cases. Therefore, we concluded that our assumption about the relationship between the suggested consequences and Kohlberg's and Gilligan's viewpoints was acceptable.

THE LOGIC OF DRAWING CONTRASTS
BETWEEN FEMALES AND MALES

Before describing ways in which the 300 females and 242 males in our survey compared along the evenhanded-justice and compassionate-caring dimension, we should make clear that when Gilligan described caring as a "different voice" from that of Kohlberg's contractual, evenhanded justice, she did not contend that she was pitting women's viewpoints against those of men. Instead, she explained:

The different voice I describe is characterized not by gender but theme. Its association with women is an empirical observation, and it is primarily through women's voices that I trace its development. But this association is not absolute, and the contrasts between male and female voices are presented here to highlight a distinction between two modes of thought and to focus a problem of interpretation rather than to represent a generalization about either sex. . . . Clearly these differences [between males' and females' perceptions] arise in a social context where factors of social status and power combine with reproductive biology to shape the experiences of males and females and the relations between the sexes (Gilligan, 1982, p. 2).

Despite this demi-disclaimer that only *theme* and not *sex* is the target of attention, the "empirical observations" and the general tenor of both the professional and popular literature about justice and caring clearly feature ostensible differences between females and males. A case in point is Noddings' book entitled *Caring*, a volume devoid of empirical data but replete with generalizations designed to:

strike many contrasts between masculine and feminine approaches to ethics and education and, indeed, to living. These are not intended to divide men and women into opposing camps. They are meant, rather, to show how great the chasm is that already divides the masculine and feminine in each of us and to suggest that we enter a dialogue of genuine dialectical nature in order to achieve an ultimate transcendence of the masculine and feminine in moral matters (Noddings, 1984, p. 6).

However, regardless of the verbiage used to mask the blunt claim of contrasts between the genders, it is apparent that writers in this field have obviously arrayed females against males in matters of moral decision. That contrast is the one we have inspected in the present study.

MALES AND FEMALES COMPARED

Table 9-1 displays the percentages of males and females who recommended the principal sanctions in the six cases of wrongdoing. Under each case, the consequences are listed in descending order from the one regarded as closest to the evenhanded-justice principle to those representing increasing degrees of compassionate caring. The table is designed to address four questions: Did more males than females advocate evenhanded justice? Did more females than males advocate compassionate options? Among observed differences between males' and females' preferences, which differences were statistically significant beyond the .05 level? Finally, to what extent are the reported differences socially significant?

Answers to the first two questions are found in the column entitled "Which Gender Is Higher?" In five of the six cases, our data bear out Gilligan's notion that males more often than females advocate evenhanded justice (as justice is defined in the present study). Furthermore, in four of the six cases the data also support the belief that females more often than males advocate compassionate caring (as caring is defined in this study). However, even though the observed differences between the two genders reflect such a pattern, in only 7—or in less than half of the 16—are the differences statistically significant at or beyond the .05 level. In short, Table 9-1 appears to reflect at least modest, though somewhat inconsistent, confirmation of Gilligan's proposal.

A question may now be asked about the import of such results for the conduct of daily life. To answer such a question, we need to shift our attention to the distinction between *statistical significance* and *social significance*. Computing the statistical significance of data enables us to estimate the probability that the observed difference between two groups actually reflects a similar difference between the two populations from which those groups were drawn. In other words, we are estimating the accuracy of our sampling and measurement procedures. However, establishing a desired level of statistical significance does not tell us whether the observed difference between the sample groups will be important in the conduct of daily social life. For guiding real-life decisions, we need a different criterion than that of statistical probability.

The term *social significance* in the present context refers to how well information about female and male differences will enable us to predict what moral values will be held by people we encounter in our daily lives. Our criterion of social significance can thus be cast as a question: "How great a difference between the genders do we require before we are willing to conclude that males and females differ markedly in their basic moral principles?" Or asked

Table 9-1

Gender Differences in Proposed Sanctions

Sanction Type	Females %	Males %	Which Gender Is Higher?	Statistically Significant?
Case 1: Colonel orders executions.				
Death	35	49	Males	.001
Life in Prison	37	29	Females	.05
Set Free	18	17	Females	—*
Case 2: Major supervises executions.				
Death	48	59	Males	.01
Life in Prison	42	29	Females	.001
Set Free	2	5	Males	—
Case 3: Girl sells drugs.				
One Year Detention	68	60	Females	—
Probation & School	19	22	Males	—
Case 4: Boy steals radio.				
One Year Detention	32	35	Males	—
Probation & School	53	57	Males	—
Case 5: Drinking male drives.				
One Year Jail	32	39	Males	—
Medical Costs & Fine	60	51	Females	.05
Suspended License	52	17	Females	.001
Case 6: Medicated female drives.				
One Year Jail	15	20	Males	—
Medical Costs & Fine	66	60	Females	—
Suspended License	23	14	Females	.01

*Percentage differences that fail to reach the .05 level are signified by
a dash (—) and are considered insignificant.

another way: "How confident can we be that the next male we meet will base
his moral judgments on evenhanded justice and that the next female we meet will
ground her moral decisions on compassionate caring?" With these questions in
mind, we can now reinspect the data in Table 9-1 that are founded on responses
of 300 females and 242 males.

In case 1, we note that 35% of the females and 49% of the males recommended that the army colonel be put to death. Furthermore, 37% of females and
29% of males recommended that he be imprisoned. Let us now assume that we
have a chance to meet some of the kinds of people who participated in the
present study. How confidently can we say that any randomly selected female we
encounter will propose imprisonment whereas any randomly chosen male will
recommend death? Are we willing to gamble that the female we meet is one of
the 37% favoring prison rather than one of the 35% who proposed death? Will
the male we meet be from the 49% suggesting death rather than from the 29%

recommending prison? Gambling on those odds seems very risky indeed. It would be quite another matter if Table 9-1 showed that 10% of the females and 90% of the males would execute the colonel, whereas 90% of the females and 10% of the males would put him in prison. In that event, we could feel quite secure in predicting which sanction would be proposed for the colonel by the next female and by the next male we might face.

Although we have used the case of the colonel to argue the importance of distinguishing between statistical and social significance, the same line of logic applies in the other five cases as well. In cases 3 and 4, the task of predicting which consequences would be suggested by females as contrasted to males would seem particularly hazardous, since the observed differences fall short of even statistical significance at the .05 level.

The point, then, is that the magnitude of the observed differences between females and males in our study is too small to warrant broad-scale conclusions about possible gender differences in the principles on which people ground their moral judgments. Perhaps—as the data for Cases 1, 2, 4, 5, and 6 indicate— there is a tendency under certain conditions for slightly more males to use evenhanded justice (as defined here) and slightly more females to employ compassionate caring (as defined here) as a foundation for moral decisions. However, it appears that some combination of other variables must play a more important role than gender in determining the kinds of moral judgments people make. Evidence from the present study, as reported in Chapters 3 through 8, suggests that the moral principles and conditions to which people subscribe are quite complex and may vary markedly from one individual to another among males and females alike. It appears that writers are guilty of generalizing far beyond the available data when they imply that gender is an accurate indicator of socially significant differences in the moral values of males and females.

CONCLUSION

To conclude, we believe that proposals of consequences for wrongdoing are founded on diverse rationales reflecting individualistic value convictions that cannot be reduced to differences of gender. In way of illustration, consider the varied proposals of consequences for the Nazi major offered by five of the females and five of the males in our opinionnaire survey.

Female A: "This man has profited from the further annihilation of even more people and should be stopped and killed for these crimes."

Female B: "While in prison he is to work on research dealing with the effects of cocaine and marijuana on society, family structures, children's lives, and infants born to addicted mothers. This is the best choice because it will hopefully give something back to humanity."

Female C: "The major should be imprisoned for five years and make financial reparations to relations/descendants. Five years at his age is crucial. He will be 73 when he gets out. Although he carried out the orders, he did not issue them but is still responsible for sadness, death, hardship, and suffering."

Female D: "He should be imprisoned with responsibility to face the survivors of those he executed, and he should be required to serve some use for the public.

I have compassion for the survivors, not for the major. I want him to have consequences which serve others, and not have life or death be easy for him."

Female E: "This man should be imprisoned, since he committed additional crimes after he left Europe. The death sentence is an easy way out. I would think it would be much worse to spend one's life in prison. I also think this man should be tried because of his crimes in South America."

Male A: "The Nazi officer should either work in a Yugoslav orphanage or die —the choice is up to him. The punishment is related to the crime of which he was convicted."

Male B: "Life imprisonment. For any crime, according to written law or not, there are consequences a perpetrator must face. I am not particularly in favor of the death penalty. I do feel that, depending on what the word 'supervised' means, his punishment might be adjusted to the degree with which he was involved in actually deciding that these people should die and in carrying it out."

Male C: "I need more information to either condemn or give amnesty. Such actions were done by Americans, Brits, Soviets during the war, so it is wrong to punish only those who committed such actions and then lost the war. Crimes of war tend to convict only those of the losing army. But he should be punished for his most recent crimes."

Male D: "He should be imprisoned, but not only that. He should be taken to schools, universities, et cetera., to speak about his crimes against humanity. He should work at trying to reverse some of the injustices he has perpetrated."

Male E: "Imprisoned for life. In many ways the former major had not paid any 'debt' to society. Despite old age, I think it is still important for that person to pay the 'debt.' I leave out the death penalty since I don't think it serves any constructive purpose."

10

Individual Styles
of Moral Reasoning

The purpose of the interview phase of our study was to illustrate diverse patterns of reasoning that could be revealed in respondents' answers to eight questions that focused directly on aspects of the taxonomy. Each interview consisted of presenting a person with one of the study's six cases of wrongdoing, along with the options for consequences that appeared on the original opinionnaire. The sequence of interview questions and the aspects of the taxonomy to which the questions related were as follows:

Interview Questions

1. What would you say was the wrong-doing in this case?
2. Which of the consequences listed below the case would you consider the best? Or perhaps you'd like to suggest some different consequences than those in this list.
3. Why do you think your choice of a consequence is a good one? That is, why did you choose your consequence rather than a different one?
4. Could this case be changed in some way that would cause you to suggest a different consequence? If so, how would you change it? And what difference would that make?
5. What do you think caused the person to commit the offense?
6. Why do you think your consequence would work?
7. What good do you think your consequence would do? What would it accomplish?

Taxonomy Aspects

1. Identification of the offense.
2. Proposed consequences.

3. Moral values, conditions, purposes, or causes that support a consequence proposal.
4. Conditions that affect the application of moral values.

5. Estimated causes of wrongdoing.
6. Causes for the expected success and feasibility of the proposed sanction.
7. Purpose of the consequence.

8. You've been willing to suggest consequences 8. Identification of qualified
   in this case. But some people aren't willing.   agents.
   They say it's not their right to propose consequences. Do you think everybody has that
   right? That is, who does and who doesn't
   have the right, and why? And who has the
   right and responsibility to see that consequences are actually carried out?

The interview results are reported under four headings: (1) methods of assessment, (2) the sample of interviewees, (3) segments of response portraits, and (4)
the significance of moral-reasoning styles.

METHODS OF ASSESSMENT

In our analysis of the audiotaped interviews, we were interested in assessing both
the content of respondents' answers and the manner in which they offered their
opinions. Thus, each interview was evaluated for both content and style.

The term *content* refers to a person's decisions as interpreted from the perspective of the taxonomy categories: (1) types of consequences, (2) moral values and
the conditions of their application, (3) purposes of consequences, (4) causes of
wrongdoing and of a consequence's expected results, (5) consequence feasibility,
and (6) who is qualified to propose consequences. The same scoring guide used
in evaluating answers in the opinionnaire-survey phase of the study was used to
score interview contents.

The term *style* refers to seven aspects of the way people cast their answers.
The first aspect, labeled *overt reasoning process*, focused on a person's apparent
mode of organizing thoughts when formulating answers. Our instrument for
rating this feature was a four-segment scale. One end of the scale was entitled
"Highly Systematic—The respondent directly enumerates all factors to be
considered, then explains each in turn." The opposite end of the scale was
entitled "Highly Groping—Most factors to be considered in forming an answer
only gradually come to mind as the respondent searches aloud. Opinions may
change during the search." The two middle segments of the scale represented two
degrees of reasoning that fell between a highly systematic process and a highly
groping process. The following examples illustrate the opposite ends of the
scale in regard to what consequences should be faced by the teenage girl who had
stabbed the teacher.

> *Highly Systematic.* "First, she should be sent to juvenile hall, where a counselor
> should try to discover what her motives were in selling pot and stabbing the
> teacher. At the same time, a social worker should investigate her home
> conditions. Was her mother a responsible parent who just couldn't cope, or
> didn't the mother really care that the girl was selling drugs? If several sessions
> of counseling the girl and her family seem to produce positive results, then the
> girl could return to her home and to school. But she would still have to be on
> probation and her behavior monitored."

> *Highly Groping.* "Oh, gosh. This is really hard. How would you know for
> sure? I really feel sorry for the girl. After all, she's still young. But then,

selling drugs and stabbing somebody is pretty bad. Of course, she could be basically okay and was just trying desperately to get money to feed the family. We wouldn't know. But carrying a knife in school—that doesn't sound very innocent. Well . . . uh . . . she does sound like a dangerous person. And I don't know if putting her in a penal institution would straighten her out. Or would psychiatric treatment help? Or what?"

The second aspect of style, *intuition versus logical argument*, focused on a respondent's apparent method of producing answers to the interview questions. An answer was deemed intuitive if the individual did not offer any line of logic or rationalized argument in support of an answer. Dependence on intuition was indicated by such a reply as: "Why is my consequence a good one? Because it's mine, the one I prefer." Or "That's just the way I feel about it. It's what I believe." In contrast, a reply was credited as logical argument when people offered a sequence of reasons as the source of their answer. Here is the sort of response that was scored as logical argument.

"You want to know why I wouldn't put the 13-year-old girl in jail for a year? Well, given the fact that the girl comes from a poor background and she has few positive figures to look up to—she has a single mother who's on welfare—I think she's being punished enough by the life style she's forced to live. I think it would be better to keep her in her familiar situation, but also have a probation officer monitor her behavior, and have some counseling support for the girl to determine what kind of life she should be leading and help her consider what should be important in her life—and not just throw her to the wolves. It would enable her to keep up with her life in school. If it's her first offense, I think she should be given this chance."

A respondent's rating along the intuition/logical-argument dimension was produced by counting the number of questions to which an intuitive answer was given as compared to the number that were supported by reasons.

The third aspect, *fertility of conditions or options*, addressed the matter of how many conditions, possibilities, or options a person included in answering a question. The unit of measurement for this dimension was the total number of conditions cited in response to questions. For instance, each underlined item in the following excerpt was judged to be a condition, so the score for this segment would be seven.

"What caused the driver to hit the women's car? Well, the incident points to his emotional state due to the fact that he's getting divorced because of his marital problems, and he's taking this out by drinking alcohol, which then affects his actions. But his divorce can't be an overriding factor to excuse him when such a serious consequence results from his actions."

The fourth aspect, *strength of ultimate conviction*, concerned an individual's apparent degree of satisfaction with the answer that he or she ultimately offered to a question. This feature was judged along a four-step scale: (1) strong conviction, quite satisfied, (2) somewhat hesitant, (3) very hesitant, not really satisfied with the answer, (4) unable to reach a decision. The four steps are illustrated with the following proposals about the cause behind the teenage boy's stealing a car stereo and hitting a police officer.

1. "He got caught and hit the cop to get away. It's that simple. He was afraid of getting caught."
2. "Maybe he'd gotten used to striking out in order to get his way. It could be that a gang he hung around with acted that way, or maybe his father used to hit him. You wouldn't know for sure, but it's probably something he learned from those around him."
3. "Well, there are lots of possibilities. He could have been startled by the officer, or maybe he just has a bad temper. He might have meant to push the officer away, and in doing so, he hit the officer with the pipe. So I guess it could have been his anger and fear. Something like that, maybe."
4. "There's no way to tell. The description of the case is awfully incomplete. There's not enough information."

The fifth characteristic, *displayed emotionality*, concerned how much expressed emotion accompanied an individual's answers. Types of feelings that might be inferred from responses included those of disapproval, anger, horror, disgust, hate, astonishment, compassion, sympathy, and the like. The evidence on which ratings were based consisted of both words and voice inflections. Typical words interpreted as implying emotion were such adjectives as *heinous, awful, unforgivable, dreadful,* and *appalling.* Types of voice inflection judged as evidence of feelings were changes in pitch, loudness, or pace that seemed to represent an affective reaction. The appraisal unit for judging emotionality was the total number of words or voice inflections judged to be signs of feelings.

The sixth feature, *self-reference*, concerned the extent to which respondents cited events in their own lives as they answered the interview questions. The unit of measurement was the number of times an interviewee displayed personal identification with some facet of the case at hand. For example, the following statements were scored as evidence of self-reference.

"I've seen how drugs have ruined people's lives. And being the mother of a teenager, I'd sure hate to see drugs brought into the country."

"I know that if someone killed my dad, I would want them to die. I never would forgive what they had done."

A final aspect, *semantic disagreement,* referred to how willingly a person agreed with the meaning of terms used by the interviewer. Most subjects accepted the interviewer's terms without comment. However, an occasional subject objected to a word or phrase, requiring that it be revised so as to reflect more accurately his or her interpretation of the case. Semantic disagreement was indicated by such comments as: "I don't want to use the word *justice*, since I think any punishment is going to be unfair to somebody. There's no really true justice, as I see it." This aspect was scored by noting the number of times a respondent amended or edited a word or phrase the interviewer had used.

The scoring of all interviews was carried out by each of us (Thomas and Diver-Stamnes) working separately. When our two sets of results were compared to determine how closely we had agreed in our appraisals, the comparison showed higher interrater reliability on certain of the style aspects than on others. For instance, we agreed 100% in judging semantic disagreement and self-reference but only 80% on fertility of conditions and 70% on emotionality.   Although there were interrater differences in the precise number of conditions or of expressions of emotionality cited, there was agreement on the general trends of these aspects. For instance, both of us agreed that Respondent C was very emotional and Respondent D quite unemotional, even though the number of "emotion units" we cited was not identical. In effect, for all seven style aspects, we agreed on the general tenor of each respondent's approach. Therefore, we concluded that our results provided sufficient grounds for creating narrative descriptions that faithfully reflected the interviewees' modes of reasoning.

In sum, each respondent's content and style ratings were used for composing a description entitled a *response portrait.* That portrait represented our effort to sketch, in brief narrative form, the essence of an individual's cognitive and affective reactions to a case of wrongdoing. The portraits give what we might answer if asked, "How does that person think, when it comes to proposing consequences for wrongdoers?"

THE SAMPLE OF INTERVIEWEES

No random, systematic, or stratified sampling procedure was followed for selecting interviewees. This was because the purpose of the interviews was not to extract generalizations that would then be applied to a larger population from which the sample was drawn. Rather, the purpose was to illustrate how the eight interview questions might elicit the varied thought patterns that marked individuals' ways of reasoning about consequences. Thus, we judged that it would be sufficient if we selected respondents with whom we were acquainted and who were willing to contribute 15 or 20 minutes to the activity. In short, our sampling method was one of availability and convenience.

The 20 interview subjects—11 females and 9 males—were from various sections of California; 14 were adults ranging in age from 22 to 65, and the remaining 4 were two 9-year-old girls and two 12-year-old boys.

The interviews, which lasted an average of 14 minutes each, were recorded on audiotape so the content and style of participants' answers could later be analyzed in detail.

SEGMENTS OF RESPONSE PORTRAITS

As noted above, the system for scoring the content and style of interviews produced data that could be used for writing brief sketches of respondents' modes of reasoning. The following dozen sketches are segments of portraits selected to demonstrate several aspects of individuals' thought patterns. The sketches are presented in contrasting sets. Each set features one or more notable differences in a given pair of participants' ways of reacting to the interview questions.

Groping and Doubtful Versus
Systematic and Assured

The first pair highlight two dimensions of style—the systematic/groping aspect and the self-assurance/self-doubt aspect.

In judging overt reasoning processes, we were able to rate the general nature of each interview at some juncture along the scale that extended from highly systematic to highly groping. However, within any given interview, an individual's manner of reasoning might not be entirely the same from one question to another. A person whose reasoning process was generally groping might be more systematic in answering one or two questions, whereas someone who was generally systematic might occasionally vacillate and struggle over a particular question.

When we appraised respondents' levels of self-assurance, we considered two characteristics of style. The first was essentially the same as the systematic/ groping aspect. A systematic approach was interpreted as reflecting self-assurance during the process of answering, whereas a groping approach was considered a sign of self-doubt. The second feature concerned how satisfied respondents were with their answer to a question, once they had arrived at a final decision. Although highly systematic respondents usually appeared satisfied with their final answers, this was not invariably so. No matter how systematic they had been in their approach, some expressed doubts about whether their final answer was adequate. Furthermore, occasionally those people who had laboriously groped toward a solution seemed ultimately pleased with their final choice.

The way these variables could form individual response profiles is demonstrated in the portraits of Subjects A and B.

Subject A: Groping and Doubtful. Throughout much of the interview, this 62-year-old woman's remarks revealed a way of reasoning that wavered and shifted as she searched for satisfactory answers. Such a pattern appeared immediately at the outset of the interview when she was asked to select a consequence for the Nazi colonel who had ordered the execution of Yugoslav partisans. After an initial pause (indicated here by three dots), she said:

> ". . . Well, I think it would be very difficult, because this man has been . . . away 37 years, and, you know, that's a strange thing. But I still think that even though . . . it says he's sick . . . it still doesn't . . . that doesn't overcome the fact that he did all this killing. So . . . I don't like to see people put to death . . . but I think that he even should be imprisoned, or there has to be something. You can't just say go on back home. That's wrong, too . . . . So many people killed. But if I had to choose among these options, I think he should be imprisoned. First, because of his age . . . . I don't want to put anybody to death, so I shouldn't say that, then. Uh . . . going back to South America is a fine thing for him, and I don't think that's deserved, do you? . . . Something has to be done. You just can't pat him on the back and send him off to South America."

Later, when the interviewer asked if there were some way the case could be changed so as to warrant a different consequence, Subject A said she did feel rather sorry for the colonel "in that he's sick and so forth." When the interviewer asked if the man's illness made a difference in the consequence he should face, the woman answered:

"Well, no, I don't think it does, because there are people who have suffered more than that. No, I don't think so. He was tried in court, and they found him guilty of all the killings, so he has to pay."

In contrast to her struggling for answers to most questions, her estimate of what caused the colonel to order the killings was immediate and emphatic.

"Because of World War Two. The Germans did this over and over and over. He wasn't the only one, you know. They killed and killed and it made no difference —women, children, it didn't matter. So he was just one part of it. He probably at one time was a really nice person, but apparently the Germans just thought that they could do anything they wanted . . . . It was because of the army itself. These people became so engrossed in what they were doing that they thought killing was a great thing."

However, when she was asked why she thought imprisoning the colonel would work, the thread of doubt that ran through most of her replies appeared again.

"Oh, I don't know that it would particularly work. It would just be that he'd feel that he's paying for the fact that he's not going to return to South America . . . he's not going to live that way any more. He may only live a few years. Something like that. But something has to be done."

Faced with the final question about whether everybody has the right to propose consequences for wrongdoing, her style of responding was consistent with the general tenor of her reasoning process throughout most of the interview. That process included searching through possibilities that came to mind at the moment, weighing the possibilities, often wavering, and occasionally expressing a measure of doubt.

"Um . . . yes, I think everybody has that right . . . . They don't particularly have the right to see that it's done, but they have the right to feel this way or that way. As for really deciding what is actually to be done, it depends on the country. Like here everybody talks [*she laughs*], everybody opens their mouth. But still, in any country there are just a few that designate this sort of thing. I don't think I would have that right, but I have the right to say what I think should happen. But who would really decide? Hm . . . it's part and parcel of the government, but I don't know actually who. Maybe, probably . . . I wonder . . . well, that's just up to whoever's in charge."

Subject B: Systematic and Assured. The case of wrongdoing in this instance was that of the recently divorced man who was involved in an auto accident. At the opening of the interview, Subject B, a 43-year-old man, first pondered for a few moments. Then he established his general style by the consequence he recommended for the motorist who drove after drinking at a bar.

"Definitely the driver's license taken away. I don't feel the man should go to jail, but I think there should be something else. And paying the medical expenses of the injured woman, yes, I agree with that. And pay the fine. But I also think there should be some type of community service, maybe related to alcohol and drug abuse, where this man would work with the victims of this type of thing. Some type of community service in lieu of jail."

When Subject B was then asked why his proposed consequences would be the best, his answer was again immediate and structured.

"Well, the way jails are constituted, I don't think he's going to come out of that situation a more productive member of society and have learned what we would want him to learn. I think if he does the community work, he's doing something that he's going to gain from. He has liability when it comes to these women, since he is responsible for causing their injuries. And a fine, that's like a fine to society that he's paying for his actions. And since he's going to lose his driver's license, he's going to be handicapped where he'll have to make adjustments to his usual work schedule and other activities. So I think he's going to learn from all these consequences."

In contrast to the promptness of his initial replies, Subject B hesitated a few moments when asked how the case might be changed to warrant a different consequence. When he did respond, he struggled more than he had when answering earlier questions.

"Hm . . . Well, I think that the seriousness of the injuries would be a factor. If people were killed in the accident, I'd have to take another look at this. And I'd have to consider some type of jail sentence. I'm very hesitant to do that, but I think in an accident where there were fatal injuries, you'd have to have jail, just as a deterrent, maybe. I'd have to think about that a lot. I'm not really clear on that. But I do think that the extent of the injuries would be a factor . . . yeah."

Subject B returned to his direct, systematic style as he addressed the matter of what had likely caused the auto accident. His approach involved prefacing his ultimate answer with a recital of events in the case and a statement of his own convictions about people's responsibilities to society.

"Well, the incident points to his emotional state, due to the fact that he's getting divorced, so he had his marital problems, which are affecting his emotional state. He's taking this out by drinking alcohol, which then affects his actions. It all comes back to the divorce and his emotional state because of that. But that can't be an overriding factor when a serious consequence like an accident takes place. There still have to be consequences, no matter what put him in this mental state. His own personal problems can't take overriding importance in determining the price he'll have to pay. Especially with alcohol, in this day and age, people have a responsibility to understand the risk of alcohol, especially when they then go out behind the wheel of an automobile. He made a conscious decision to have the alcohol and to drive, so he has to take the consequences for what happened."

Subject B's approach to the remaining questions assumed this same pattern—an orderly, detailed recounting of conditions and supporting arguments that led to a solution with which he seemed satisfied.

Among interviewees who appeared systematic and assured, we noted two varieties of style. Some paused before answering, apparently to organize their thoughts. Others answered immediately, giving the impression that they already had in mind a well-structured rationale, or else they were able spontaneously to generate a convincing line of logic as they spoke. Therefore, because our assessment method focused solely on interviewees' overt responses, we were unable to distinguish respondents who already had answers in mind from those who promptly created a line or argument on the spot.

Highly Emotional and Emphatic Versus Unemotional and Hesitant

The overt display of feelings not only varied from one respondent to another, but it also frequently varied among the segments of a single interview, as demonstrated in the following vignettes.

Subject C: Much Emotion. The strain of strong emotional involvement that would course through the interview session appeared first in this 35-year-old woman's suggestion of a proper consequence to be experienced by the Nazi major who had supervised the killing of Yugoslav partisans.

"I'd put him to death. Or my sick, sadistic side would say maybe we could give him one of those nice little showers of gas and then invite the families of the victims. This may sound silly, but really I can't think of anything bad enough. Death almost seems too easy. I'm not sure I would want to torture the person, but I guess I would want him to learn a hell of a lesson and then be killed. I don't care how old he is. I wish he were younger so we could put him in prison for a long time and then kill him. The drug dealing is bad, but my rage is toward the killing. As a person, he's pond scum."

When asked why she regarded her proposed consequence to be the best option, she replied:

"Now as I think about it, maybe putting him in prison with someone who really hates Germans might be better. Let him just sit there and rot . . . . But then again, it probably would be best to put him to death. It's like an eye for an eye."

In explaining why she thought the major had participated in the slayings, she said:

"Even with Americans in wartime, their morals change a bit, so their response is like . . . well, I've talked to women who've said that during the war they would go to bed with men that normally they wouldn't go to bed with, and then they say, 'Well, it was war time.' Now what the hell is that! In the same way, soldiers do whatever they think is good for the cause. And maybe that's how the Nazi officer was."

The emotional content of her answers was matched by alterations in voice inflections—a rise and fall in pitch and volume—and by an intermittent quickening and slowing in the pace of delivery. This mode was accompanied by an emphatic commitment to the answers she offered.

Subject D: Slight Emotion. In contrast to the strong emotional tone of the 35-year-old woman's replies was the even-tempered mood of a 64-year-old man as he addressed the case of the girl who was caught selling drugs in school. Not only did he make sparse use of affect-laden terms, but his delivery throughout was monotonic, devoid of pitch and pacing inflections. Such a pattern began with his comments about the consequences the girl should experience for her actions.

> "A person who stabs someone with a knife should not be returned to society with no corrective action taken. Selling marijuana is not right according to our laws, but I don't think it's going to kill anybody. And in her circumstances, I guess any way to get money is a way to get money. So you could easier overlook the sale of marijuana than you could the stabbing, which is something that makes her a potentially dangerous person. And I don't know if putting her in a penal institution is going to straighten her out, or psychiatric help would help her, or what. But she shouldn't be allowed to continue in the same manner without some sort of corrective action being taken."

As his remarks demonstrate, Subject D was unwilling to commit himself to a specific consequence. Periodically during the interview he paused, head down, looking at the floor in apparent concentration. Once the interview was over and the tape recorder turned off, he remained quiet for a moment, then looked up and began to speak freely about why he felt he could not assign a consequence for the girl's actions. He said he needed much more information, including a social worker's analysis of the girl's family life, reports of her performance in school, and a personality profile prepared by a psychologist.

Although throughout the interview the general tone of Subject D's approach was unemotional, on a few occasions the phrases he used revealed feelings he held about the case.

> "A little marijuana dealer like this girl is not going to hurt anybody. But if she was a big dealer and had kilos and kilos of it, then *wham*, incarcerate her for the rest of her life."
>
> "Everyone has the right to express an opinion about what consequences people should face. But thank God I'm not a judge and don't have to decide what actually is done."

The fact that the foregoing pair of cases contrasts a high emotional display by a woman with a low display by a man should not be interpreted to mean that all the females we interviewed showed their feelings more than did the males. Some of the males appeared more emotional than some of the females. In effect, the level of emotion seemed more a characteristic of individual personalities and of possible individual reactions to participating in tape-recorded interviews than it was a trait more associated with one gender or the other.

Simple and Conclusive versus Complex and Indecisive

The word *simple* in this context applies to respondents who considered only a limited number of conditions while arriving at an answer, and they identified few if any interactions among conditions. In contrast, *complex* means that respondents suggested multiple conditions, and they specified the interactions among conditions that would affect their answers.

The term *conclusive* means that when people finally arrive at an answer, they seem satisfied and committed to it. *Indecisive* refers to a reluctance to offer a particular solution to a problem or to be satisfied with whatever solution they may ultimately suggest.

Subjects E and F were both judging the case of the 13-year-old girl who was caught selling marijuana in school.

Subject E: Simple and Conclusive. Although this 12-year-old boy paused occasionally to ponder a question before he answered, in general he replied promptly. Furthermore, his answers tended to be rather simple, in that they did not involve a variety of conditions to be considered in arriving at a solution. When asked which of the printed consequences he would propose, he replied:

"I don't like any of them. But can I make up my own? Well, she might spend a couple of months in juvenile detention to see what it was like and then be on probation for a long time. If she does anything wrong in that time, then she'll go back to detention for a year so she can learn not to do that kind of stuff."

When asked what he thought caused the girl to sell drugs and to knife the teacher, he said:

"The way she did it sounds like she was a vicious person. There's something in her life that's totally wrong."

Furthermore, Subject E tended to consider one factor at a time, somewhat independent of others, until the factors' interrelations were brought to his attention. In suggesting ways the case might be altered to influence his proposed consequence, he said:

"If she didn't stab the person, then you could put her in juvenile detention for a week or so and tell her, 'Don't do this again or there'll be stronger consequences.' Or tell her, 'We'll let you go this time, but if we catch you doing it again there'll be worse consequences.'"

When the interviewer next asked, "So selling marijuana is a lot less serious, in your opinion, than the stabbing?" he answered:

"Uh, well, I'm not going to say it's a lot less. I'm probably going to have the same consequences, since marijuana can do a lot more damage to more people, while the stabbing does damage to just one . . . . Yeah, the consequences could be the same for both the marijuana and the stabbing."

Another characteristic of Subject E's style was the conclusiveness of his solutions. Once he settled on an answer, he appeared quite confident that his proposal was sound.

"I think my idea is good because she'll learn to behave, and she'll know that she'll be in more trouble if she does it again."

Subject F: Complex and Indecisive. A dominant theme that typified this 44-year-old man's manner throughout the interview was signaled by his opening remark after he had read the case of the girl who stabbed the teacher:

"These are complicated societal problems and, unfortunately, there are no easy answers."

The doubt reflected in this comment would subsequently appear in other answers. For instance, in proposing a consequence, he first said:

"I'm very uncomfortable with just sending her to juvenile detention. If somehow there was a very fine program that would help her raise her self-esteem, her expectations in life, and her abilities to cope with life, then that might be the best way to deal with it."

He also suggested that the girl's family needed some sort of therapy:

"I would suspect that the family situation is the core of a whole lot of the problem.   But again, I'm not optimistic, knowing our society, that the type of support and program that would be needed to help this family would be in place. They need some sort of program, not to punish, but to change their life situation and the individuals' outlook."

As we tried to account for Subject F's pattern of response, we speculated that his diffidence perhaps resulted from three features of his moral-reasoning style. First, we assumed that he believed human behavior is very complex, determined by a multiplicity of factors that are hard to specify and whose relative influence is difficult to judge.

"In the long term it's what's effective for preventing her from recommitting these offenses, and at the same time how do you get her to the point of being a contributing member of the society."

Second, we estimated that he regarded his knowledge of certain influential factors as being too meager to guide him toward a sound solution.   His comments were occasionally accompanied by such phrases as, "From what little I know about detention systems, and it's not very much, . . ." or "We don't know what's going on in the home."

Third, we presumed that in his particular value system he was reluctant to accord one moral principle greater power than certain other principles. As a consequence, he appeared to reach a decision-making impasse whenever two principles of equal force were pitted against each other. For instance, he often cited two opposing values or conditions to which he seemed to give equal weight; and the resulting conflict appeared to thwart his attempt to provide a conclusive answer.

"There have to be consequences for behavior. So it's not like this young woman should get the message that what she did is all right. You don't want her to endanger other people. Maybe you need to keep her [in detention] for 24 hours a day for a while to prevent her from engaging in this behavior. On the other hand, this type of thing concerns me tremendously. She has a whole potential for life in front of her. If she could be influenced by the right program, it could turn her life around, and she could succeed in being a positive, happy member of society.

"Then there's the question: What if the teacher had died? I'm really not sure how to respond to that. Whether he died or not—it seems like there's not too much difference in terms of what the girl's intention and action were. But of course there's a big difference in the impact on the victim and his family. If you're going to try to stab somebody with a knife, whether you just wound them or you kill them is kind of the-luck-of-the-draw."

Self-Reference and Many Conditions Versus Objectivity and Few Conditions

The first dimension of style featured in the following portraits is that of self-reference versus objectivity. As noted earlier, people often differ in the degree to which they overtly identify with conditions in cases of wrongdoing. Some imagine themselves in the shoes of either the offender or the victim, whereas others distance themselves from personal involvement with any features of the case. In the present study, we rated interviewees on this dimension by the number of times they referred to their own lives and by the amount of emotion they expressed.

Fertility of conditions is the second aspect of style featured in the following vignettes. It's important to recognize that people who make frequent references to themselves do not necessarily cite many conditions, nor do those who distance themselves from personal identification with a case necessarily cite few conditions. But such a pairing of those two aspects just happened to occur in the interviews with Subjects G and H, illustrating something about each respondent's individualistic style. Other interviews resulted in quite different patterns of self-reference and fertility.

Subject G: Self-Reference and Many Conditions. Subject G, a 46-year-old man, cited numerous conditions in qualifying his answer to nearly every question. For instance, in proposing sanctions for the motorist who had stopped by a bar and later crashed into another car, Subject G suggested:

> "The man should pay a $1,000 fine and pay the medical costs of the women who were injured in the crash. I think he should also do some jail time. But I thought the first option—a year in jail—is a long time for what may be a first offense. Yet if he only has to pay a fine and medical costs, depending on his income, it may be too easy for him just to write a check. So I think a little time behind bars will make a bigger impression—maybe two months or weekends for six months—but a whole year is a bit excessive. Another of the options—taking away his driver's license for a year—isn't enough for what he did."

Subject G's habit of embellishing his proposals with numerous qualifications was also evident in his reply to the question about what sorts of changes in the case might warrant a different consequence.

> "The description says he drove after he had several drinks of whisky, but that doesn't necessarily mean he was intoxicated. By legal definition in California, the alcohol level in the blood is .08, I think. It's hard for me to believe he wasn't intoxicated after having several drinks, but that is a possibility. Maybe he wasn't legally drunk. So whether he was drunk driving or just reckless makes a difference in what consequences he should face. Drunk driving is different than just running a stop sign because your mind is preoccupied. But I've assumed he was drunk.

"The case would also be different if the women had been killed as opposed to being seriously injured. The courts would say it was manslaughter, and that might then lead me toward recommending jail for at least a year.

"I don't think the fact that his wife was divorcing him excuses his behavior. It may have been the reason he was drinking, but it is not an excuse for drunk driving."

At this point, Subject G connected conditions of the case with events in his own life.

"Another thing that might change the proposed consequences is the matter of how visible is the stop sign. Sometimes people go through stop signs whether they are sober or drunk because the sign has been obstructed by a bush, or maybe a new stop sign is put up where there didn't used to be one. I've done that myself, where I didn't realize that all of a sudden there's a four-way stop where there used to be a two-way stop. That would be a mitigating circumstance—he could have missed the stop sign even if he had been sober."

Self-reference appeared again when Subject G was asked about what apparently was the cause of the motorist's misdeed.

"I'm assuming the drinking and/or anger. It's possible that he drank because he was angry over the divorce. I would have been angry myself, but I wouldn't have been drinking over it."

When asked why he thought his proposed consequences would deter the motorist in the future from driving after drinking, Subject G said:

"I think the jail time would make more of an impression than having to put out money for the fine and medical costs. The whole idea is to get the person to think of his actions the next time around. I know there are some programs where they have you go down and watch an autopsy of a person who's been killed by a drunk driver. That may or may not have an effect. But I know for me, time behind bars every weekend would give me a lot of time to think."

In reply to the question about who is qualified to suggest consequences for wrongdoing, Subject G said that as a private citizen he had as much right as anyone else to make recommendations. However, in regard to who has the right to determine the sanctions that actually will be carried out, he said:

"I, as a jury of one, don't have the right to decide for this particular person— well, that he should have his head cut off. I'd like to hear the opinions of some other people. They might be able to rebut my opinion and maybe have a better solution than I. So I think it should be done by a committee or court of law. I have a right to voice my opinion about what would be a just consequence, yet I wouldn't want my opinion to be the deciding factor. Unless, of course, I was a judge elected by the people."

Subject H: Abstract Objectivity and Few Conditions. Subject H, a 35-year-old woman, discussed the case of the boy who had stolen a car radio and hit a police officer. Whereas Subject G had alluded to conditions in his own life as he proposed consequences, Subject H made no such references. Her delivery was marked by prompt, assured replies expressed in a level voice that was devoid of alterations in pitch or pacing emphasis. While she appeared sympathetic with the boy's plight, her approach appeared to be an objective analysis of someone else's situation, which was not a situation in which she vicariously placed herself.

"As for consequences, I would go for the second option—have him put in a foster home, enrolled in school, and see a probation officer on a regular basis. I chose this because juvenile detention facilities, in my understanding, are not good places for children to be. They don't help the situation at all—in fact, they make it worse. Although a foster home is not an ideal situation, it does give the opportunity for some structure, hopefully a caring environment. And putting him in school gives him a background of knowledge that could enable him in later years to go out into the world, get a job, and build a good life for himself."

A further way in which the interview style of Subject H differed from that of Subject G was in the number of conditions or options cited in answering a question. Whereas Subject G had cited many conditions, Subject H suggested no more than two or three options in her answer to any of the questions. For example, when asked how the case of the boy might be changed so as to warrant a different consequence, she suggested:

"If the boy's parents had not put him out on the street and they really cared about him, then I would consider his biological family environment superior to a foster home."

Likewise, when asked the likely cause of the boy's misbehavior, she offered two options:

"There are a few possibilities. One could be he needed the money from the sale of the car radio to feed himself, because he was out on the street. There's also the possibility that he was very angry with his parents and did this to get their attention."

In describing the purpose her suggested consequence might accomplish, Subject H limited her expected outcomes to stability and structure:

"In the foster home he would be in a more stable family environment than being out on the street and in school, so that could put structure back into his life and give him something to hold on to."

The interview closed with Subject H considering who would be qualified to propose consequences in such a case.

"Everyone is entitled to an opinion. But in actually carrying out the consequences, I think that the boy's parents should be involved; and probably a judge for juveniles as well as the boy should have a say. He's 13 years old. He's old enough to realize he's done something wrong. These people should get together and exchange views. But probably the judge should ultimately make the decision."

To summarize, the analysis of the case offered by Subject H featured a mixture of objective appraisal and of concern for the boy's right to participate in deciding the consequences he would face.

Intuitive Choices Versus Explicit Principles and Rationalized Conditions

As noted earlier, an individual's answer was scored as *intuitive* if the person failed to offer a line of reasoning in support of the answer. On the other hand, an answer was credited as *logical argument* if reasons were provided.

In the following pair of examples, Subject I occasionally avoided giving reasons—other than general feelings—for her answers, even when asked to do so. On the other hand, Subject J not only stated the moral principles behind her decisions but always explained which conditions affected her judgments.

Subject I: Intuitive Choices. After this 43-year-old woman suggested that the Nazi colonel who had ordered the Yugoslavs' execution should spend life in prison, she was asked why she thought her proposal was the most suitable.

> "Because that's what I feel most comfortable with. I'm not comfortable with the death penalty; but he deprived people of their lives, so he should be made to pay, even though he's old and sick. That's just the feeling I have, right or wrong. I just don't like the idea of the guy getting away with it. That's my feeling."

In contrast to this rather weakly supported choice was the woman's reaction to the question about how the case might be changed to warrant a different consequence. Here she did provide a more reasoned supporting argument.

> "If he weren't so ill and so old, I might consider having him work with people who might need his help. You know, do volunteer work for a number of years, serving people rather than killing them, because prison is often very stale and unproductive."

Subject J: Explicit Principles and Rationalized Conditions. The subject was a 23-year-old woman discussing the case of the Nazi major who had supervised the execution of the Yugoslavs. Her style consistently featured an explanation of the moral principles and conditions that were the source of her judgments. She began by contrasting the principle of "regard for human life" with that of "role-suitable behavior," then stated that in her own philosophy she valued regard for life over role suitability or loyalty to a cause. When asked if the case involved wrongdoing, she said:

> "This is tough, because in a war the rules are a little different, since you're fighting your enemy. So what this man did in terms of the army was right. But in terms of my personal moral law, it was very wrong."

When asked what consequence she would propose for the major, she struggled with conflicts that she said were yet unresolved in her value system, including a conflict between expenses born by society and the morality of capital punishment.

> "Okay, my personal moral law would probably have me leaning between prison and death, because I haven't answered the question inside myself as to whether capital punishment is a good way to go. I have a problem with putting someone to death—with taking someone's life. But if you are to completely control someone's life, like putting them in prison, you've taken their life anyway. Part

of me says you put him in prison for the rest of his life, but then you have to pay all that money to support him—unless you get the prisoners themselves to give constructive service to the community, like repairing the roads, and maybe make up for some of the crime they committed. Under those conditions prison would probably be a good solution—allow him the opportunity to make amends. But then there's the problem of the tax dollars to support him."

As she told why punishing the major was a good idea, she again described moral convictions on which she founded her decision—that violent aggression is unacceptable, that people have a right to self-determination, and that members of a group involved in wrongdoing bear responsibility for the group's actions.

"Morally I don't believe in war at all. So if these Yugoslavs were fighting for their freedom, then the Germans were killing freedom fighters; and I will have to side with those people because they have a right to their freedom. I feel that anyone who participates in orchestrating that violence deserves punishment."

In answer to the question of why the major had supervised the executions, she surmised:

"Everyone in some sense is socialized into particular roles in life, so somehow society placed him in the army role and he just played that role. Then after the war, in order to keep enjoying the good life, he had to do this other thing—drug dealing. People get driven by greed, and they do what they think necessary to have the good life. He still wanted power, so he moved from one kind of power to another."

It is of some interest to note that Subject J revealed in a passing comment that among the convictions on which she founded her answers was her belief in the concept of *karma*. From a traditional Hindu-Buddhist worldview, a person's soul is not extinguished when the person dies. Rather, the soul is transferred into a new body for an additional period of life on earth. In this transmigration, the soul carries along the total consequences of the good deeds and bad deeds that the now-departed person performed when alive. This sum of deeds (bad deeds subtracted from good ones) is the individual's *karma*, which determines the kind of new body the soul will inhabit and the fate of that new body on earth. A dominance of good deeds over bad ones portends a happy, successful new life. A preponderance of bad deeds results in the soul's encasement in the body of a less fortunate form of life—perhaps an animal—that will have a lifetime of difficulties. As Subject J explained why she thought her suggested consequence would work, she said:

"If he did something constructive for society while in prison, then the community benefits from a person whose freedom is taken away. Also, karmically you let a person work off the crimes they committed or the wrongs they've done, so you've given that person the chance to still advance in their life to a higher level karmically."

This pattern of basing her answers on a line of logic continued through the final question about who was qualified to recommend and impose consequences on wrongdoers.

Semantic Disagreement

In most interviews, the respondents accepted the apparent meaning of terms that the interviewer used. However, on rare occasion an individual objected to a word or phrase, as illustrated in the reactions of Subjects K and L.

Subject K: Right and Wrong. When Subject K, a 32-year-old man, was first asked whether there was wrongdoing in the case of the woman who had driven her car while she was under medication, he said emphatically:

"You know, I hate the terms *right* and *wrong*. They just don't do anything for me at all. It seems like the terms *right* and *wrong* just keep people from growing. Instead, I'd say there was responsibility but not . . . not wrong. Obviously the woman who was taking the drug is responsible for hitting this boy who was injured. At the same time I don't see what good it does to say that she was wrong. I think it is right to say she was responsible."

In proposing a consequence the woman driver should experience, Subject K continued to use his preferred term *responsible* and stated:

"I don't agree with any of the consequences in the list. I would say she would be responsible, but she would not be punished by law. She would have the consequence of taking care of the medical expenses if there was no other way to do it. Punishment? I've never really seen it work, whether with adults or kids. But I have seen the power behind people taking responsibility for what they've done, once they've accepted what they've done."

The interviewer inquired, "If there was another way to take care of the expenses, then there would be no consequences for the woman?" Subject K agreed. When asked how the case could be changed that would cause him to suggest a different consequence, he said:

"Well, if the scenario had nothing to do with medicine or drowsiness but she ran into this kid because she didn't like him, then I might say there's been some wrong here."

Subsequent questioning revealed the basis of Subject K's objection to the term *wrongdoing*. In his opinion, an action should be called *wrong* only if motivated by malicious intent. On the assumption that the woman had not intended to hit the bicyclist, her act should not be labeled *wrongdoing*.

Subject L: Consequences. As Subject L, a 23-year-old woman, discussed the case of the teenager who was selling marijuana, she suggested that the girl be allowed to return to her home and to school but also be required to meet weekly with a probation officer. However, a semantic disagreement arose when the interviewer asked why Subject L thought her consequence was a good one.

"Well, I didn't think of my suggestion as a consequence. A consequence sounds so negative, like if you misbehave, then this is the consequence. I guess I'm thinking of all this teacher thing— 'If you have rules, you must have consequences.' I see my suggestion more as people stepping in to help the girl. I don't think that what I chose would be a punishment, but more a supportive thing than a consequence."

THE SIGNIFICANCE OF MORAL REASONING STYLES

Our analysis of the moral reasoning styles as revealed in the interviews led us to pose this question: In daily life, what is the practical significance of differences in the reasoning styles displayed in moral situations? By exploring what the answer might be, we were able to generate the following hypotheses that could be tested in future investigations.

Two ways that overt cognitive styles may affect decisions in daily life are (1) in how thoroughly an audience is convinced that a proposed consequence is the most appropriate one and (2) in the influence that members of a decision-making group exert on each other and on the ultimate consequence produced by the group.

Convincing an Audience

The word *audience* in the present context means any group of people who hear someone suggest consequences in a case of wrongdoing. Such a group could be students listening to a teacher, ball players listening to a coach, a jury listening to a prosecuting attorney, soldiers listening to an officer, voters listening to a politician, workers listening to a boss, and the like.

From the impressions we gained while hearing the interviews in the present study, we offer the following speculation:

Hypothesis 1: People who observe an individual propose consequences for an instance of wrongdoing will more likely be persuaded that those consequences are suitable if the reasoning style of the proposer (1) is more systematic than groping, (2) is based more on rational argument than on intuition, (3) specifies the moral principles and conditions on which the consequences are founded, (4) suggests that the proposer is strongly convinced that those consequences are just, and (5) is similar to their own mode of expressing emotion and engaging in self-reference.

Of the five aspects of style in this hypothesis, the first three have been included because they can affect how precisely proposers communicate their values and logic to an audience. The fourth—level of conviction—reflects our belief that speakers are less persuasive when they seem unsure that the plan they are advocating is sound. The fifth aspect—emotionality and self-reference—is based on our assumption that a speaker's mode of expressing emotion or self-reference will be more acceptable to listeners who, in their own lives, display a similar mode of reasoning.

By offering hypothesis 1, we do not mean to suggest that the only way a proposal influences an audience is by the speaker's style of presentation. Obviously, the substance of a proposal is significant as well. Hence, it is proper to pose a second hypothesis whose validity is perhaps so apparent that it may qualify as a truism.

Hypothesis 2: Members of an audience will be persuaded of the desirability of a recommended consequence to the degree that they already agree with (1) the moral principles on which the consequence is grounded, (2) the relative importance accorded different principles that may be involved in an instance of wrongdoing, and (3) the conditions that can affect the application of the principles.

In relation to the matter of convincing an audience, it is important to distinguish between *persuasiveness* and *desirability*. It should be clear that just because a speaker's style persuades others to endorse his or her proposed consequence does not necessarily mean that such a consequence is the most desirable or appropriate. The decision about desirability and appropriateness is governed by the moral values (principles and conditions) to which a particular individual subscribes. The consequence which a convincing debater espouses may or may not reflect that individual's values. Hence, speakers often assume the guise of huckster, endeavoring to make the consequence they embrace appear to be in harmony with the values of as many members of the audience as possible.

Influencing a Group Decision

Typical groups responsible for determining consequences for wrongdoing include juries in court trials, a family considering misdeeds of its members, schools' disciplinary committees, state legislatures, city and county commissioners, and governing boards of labor unions and professional associations.

To a great extent, the effect of people's moral-reasoning style on group decision making appears much the same as the influence of style on an audience. Therefore, we estimate that the two hypotheses listed above also pertain to instances of group decision making. However, there are at least two important differences between an audience and a decision-making group. First, an audience is composed of passive listeners, whereas members of a decision-making body are active participants who may influence each other's roles in determining the consequence that the group recommends. Second, members of a decision-making body usually bear direct responsibility for the fate that a wrongdoer will actually experience, whereas members of an audience do not.

To help account for the kinds of consequences that derive from group judgments, we estimate that three personality traits of individual members will significantly influence the decision-making process. The three are seen as dimensions or scales on which an individual's general mode of interpersonal behavior can be located.

The first is a *dominant-submissive* scale, which concerns how likely a person will urge his or her beliefs on others or, in contrast, how likely a person will yield to the demands of others.

Hypothesis 3: In group decisions about consequences, individuals whose interpersonal style is higher in dominance will exert greater effect on the consequences ultimately submitted by the group than will individuals whose style is more submissive.

The second dimension is labeled *ease of persuasion*. Although this is similar to the dominant-submissive scale, the two are not identical. A person who submits to another's opinions or desires can do so for either of two reasons. First, an individual may yield to a powerful person without really being convinced that the advocate's opinions are right; this is an instance of intimidation. Or second, the submission can result from the dominant individual adducing such persuasive reasons in support of a consequence that the submissive person accepts the consequence as proper. Hence, to care for this second possibility, our fourth hypothesis is founded on the belief that people vary in terms of how easily they are persuaded to adopt others' views

Hypothesis 4: People who, in general, are easily persuaded by a line of reasoning will more likely adopt the opinions of others than are people who, in general, remain unmoved when confronted with a line of reasoning about consequences that is intended to alter their original opinion.

The third scale concerns *willingness to act*. This trait came to the fore during our interviews when respondents were asked who they believed had the right to suggest sanctions and who would be responsible for seeing that those sanctions were carried out. In a number of instances, interviewees were willing to suggest consequences but admitted that they would be unwilling, or at least very hesitant, to take responsibility for seeing that such sanctions were actually applied under real-life conditions. This reluctance was reflected in such comments as:

"I really wouldn't want to send anyone to jail, even though that might be the best thing for protecting society. I wouldn't want the girl's whole life balancing on my judgment."
"If the offender was right there before me and this judgment had to be made . . . well, I've often tried to get out of jury duty because it's a hard thing to do."
"Who has the right to make the final determination? My God, I wouldn't want to be that person."

However, other respondents' remarks implied that they would be more prone to act on their stated convictions under real-life circumstances.

"We have to be ready to take part in making these decisions rather than abdicate that role. Otherwise, we don't have a justice system that we have created."

The notion of willingness-to-act suggests a final hypothesis.

Hypothesis 5: People vary in their willingness to participate in implementing proposed consequences. Those who are most reluctant (1) will recommend more lenient sanctions than they might have proposed if they were not involved in putting the sanctions into practice and (2) will later place the blame for harsh sanctions on other members of the decision-making group, especially if the sanctions appear to be unpopular.

CONCLUSION

The primary aim of this chapter has been to illustrate seven aspects of reasoning style that we extracted from interviews in which people recommended consequences for wrongdoers. The seven were labeled overt reasoning process, intuitive versus logical argument, fertility of conditions, strength of ultimate conviction, displayed emotionality, self-reference, and semantic disagreement.

A secondary aim has been to suggest the role that reasoning style plays in convincing an audience of the suitability of a proposed consequence and in influencing the members of a group that is determining consequences for people who committed misdeeds.

Part IV

Postscript

To finish this volume's report of the just-deserts investigation, Part IV offers a single chapter called "An Overview, Applications, and Research Prospects." As its title suggests, the chapter first summarizes principal findings derived from the project. The discussion next turns to practical ways that the taxonomy in Part II might be used. Finally, the chapter closes with suggestions about further research topics to be pursued in the realm of moral reasoning about consequences for wrongdoers.

11

An Overview, Applications, and Research Prospects

The overview that opens Chapter 11 focuses on primary outcomes of our investigation and describes some of our personal reactions to those outcomes. The second portion of the chapter suggests ways the taxonomy may be applied as either an instructional tool or an evaluation device in several life situations. The chapter closes with a discussion of further research possibilities that can be pursued along the route taken in the present study.

THE OVERVIEW

The dual aim of this research project was (1) to derive a taxonomy of moral reasoning from the answers that 542 students offered in an opinionnaire survey and (2) to use the taxonomy as the basis for comparing six groups of respondents and for analyzing the overt moral-reasoning styles of 20 additional individuals whom we interviewed. The following summary first describes the development of the taxonomy, then reports representative findings derived from comparing groups and individuals in terms of the taxonomy's contents.

Constructing the Taxonomy

Three of the six groups that contributed to the opinionnaire survey were from institutions on the U.S. West Coast: (a) Polk-Metro Public High School, located in an economically depressed, high-crime-rate district of a large city (132 participants); (b) San Pablo Parochial High School, situated in a small, prosperous city (166 participants); and (c) Northcoast University, whose teacher-education program furnished the 63 graduate students that took part in the survey. Two other groups were in the state of Hawaii at (d) Makai Public High School, which enrolled students from relatively low-income families living in the small seacoast town of Makai (31 participants); and (e) Pele Community College on the outskirts of the state's largest urban center (24 participants). The sixth group was composed of 44 high school students and 82 university students attending institutions in one of Saudi Arabia's major cities. The 20 people who engaged in the interview portion of the investigation were from various regions of California and ranged in age from 9 to 65 years.

The task assigned to participants in the opinionnaire survey was that of suggesting the consequences that offenders in six cases of wrongdoing should face and of explaining why they considered those consequences appropriate.

In the first phase of the data analysis, we inspected students' answers on the 542 opinionnaires to determine the types of categories into which answers might be placed to reveal the participants' modes of moral reasoning about consequences for wrongdoers. Whereas all 126 Saudi Arabian students recommended consequences in the six cases, very few chose to explain why they selected such measures. Therefore, the major contributors to the analysis of moral-reasoning patterns were the 416 American students, most of whom wrote rationales in support of their consequence choices.

Our analysis resulted in five major taxonomy categories described as (a) moral values, consisting of principles and conditions of their application; (b) consequence purposes; (c) causes of wrongdoing and of consequence effectiveness; (d) feasibility considerations; and (e) agent qualifications.

In composing the moral-values category, we supplemented the moral principles implied in the opinionnaire responses with additional principles found in a one-month informal review of items from local newspapers and from television and radio newscasts. This process resulted in 30 moral principles divided among four subcategories entitled: general societal obligations (10), affective regard for others (9), personal rights (6), and sexual relations (5). Twenty-three of the principles were extracted from the opinionnaires and the remaining seven from daily news items.

All 44 of the conditions affecting the application of moral principles were derived from the analysis of the 542 opinionnaires. They were organized within eight sets labeled: character traits (5), prior circumstances (2), concurrent circumstances (15), post-incident circumstances (12), fair chance (4), extent of damage (4), legal status of the behavior (1), and value compatibility (1).

In the process of analyzing the students' responses, we were surprised at how many different moral principles appeared in participants' reactions to only three pairs of cases. We were even more amazed at the large number of different conditions that were either stated outright or implied in the rationales respondents wrote in defense of their proposed sanctions and treatments.

Purposes that respondents hoped their consequences would achieve appeared on around two-thirds of the opinionnaires. From our inspection of students' responses, we identified 26 purposes which we placed within a hierarchy consisting of three levels: ultimate outcomes (15), instrumental goals (4), and implementing purposes (7).

Our examination of opinionnaires to discover students' beliefs about causality showed that very few directly addressed matters of cause in their written rationales. Thus, it was necessary to infer their ideas of causality from what they had written about other matters. We viewed notions of causality from four perspectives—those of proximate versus underlying factors, heredity-environment interactions, a causal process, and people's motives.

A relatively small number of participants cited feasibility considerations as the reason they preferred one consequence over another. The five categories adopted for organizing types of feasibility were labeled unacceptable side effects, funds, facilities, personnel, and effectiveness of goal achievement.

The final component of the taxonomy centered on the issue of which individuals or organizations were qualified to propose consequences. We identified six types of agents that might be considered appropriate—a supreme being, the natural course of events, a government agency, a religious body, peers, and the family.

Group and Individual Comparisons

When the structure of the taxonomy was complete, we reanalyzed the 542 opinionnaires in order to score the students' responses in terms of the taxonomy's categories. A central purpose of this scoring phase was to discover how the choices of one group compared with those of another. The results reported in Chapters 6 through 9 led us to the following conclusions.

There were marked differences of opinion among the respondents within any given group. That is, in any of the groups, the members expressed a wide variety of proposals about suitable consequences, moral principles, conditions affecting the application of principles, the purposes of consequences, and estimated causes of wrongdoing. Thus, in terms of moral reasoning, the groups lacked homogeneity. Instead, each group's members displayed a diversity of individual values.

The differences between one group and another were relatively few. In other words, the similarities between groups were greater than the differences. This finding came to us as a considerable surprise. When we had originally selected survey participants, we had purposely chosen groups that represented identifiably diverse cultural contexts. We surmised that students living in a metropolitan district that was notable for its high incidence of crime, unemployment, and poverty would display significantly different attitudes toward consequences for misdeeds than would students attending a church-sponsored high school in a prosperous, low-crime-rate small city. We imagined that even greater differences would be found between Saudi Arabian students and ones in U.S. American cultural settings. However, such expectations were, in general, not supported by the survey results.

In view of the conspicuous within-group heterogeneity, coupled with the high incidence of intergroup similarities, we recognized that it is a very risky venture to try guessing a student's moral values simply by knowing the group from which that student comes. In effect, knowing a respondent's group tells little or nothing about what his or her opinions will be regarding appropriate consequences for wrongdoers.

However, the fact that there were greater similarities than differences between groups does not mean that the groups were entirely identical. For example, Northcoast University graduate students tended to be more lenient in the consequences they proposed than were members of the other five groups. Saudi Arabians proposed harsher sanctions for the drug-dealing former Nazi major and more compassionate treatment of the teenage boy who stole a car radio than did members of the five American groups. Furthermore, greater initiative in devising consequences was demonstrated by Northcoast University respondents than by any other group. The students who showed the least inventiveness in creating consequence choices were those from Polk-Metro High and Makai High. San Pablo Parochial students and those at Pele Community College scored between the Northcoast group and the Polk-Metro and Makai respondents on initiative. These results proved to be highly correlated with students' skill in communicating their ideas in writing. As a group, Northcoast graduate students wrote more in defense of their consequence proposals and made fewer writing errors than did members of the other groups. Polk-Metro and Makai respondents wrote the least and made the greatest number of writing errors. San Pablo and Pele students fell between these extremes.

In seeking to account for such differences, we speculated that the cause might be a combination of (a) differences in the groups' language environments and past learning opportunities, (b) the kinds of learning opportunities that either the students' parents or the students themselves are able to choose, (c) the motivation for pursuing such opportunities, and (d) the selective function of the schooling hierarchy that eliminates less promising scholars as they reach the more advanced steps of the formal-education ladder.

In addition to comparing groups that represented six different cultural settings and different age and schooling levels, we also compared the responses of the 300 females with those of the 242 males who participated in the survey. Contrary to an expectation that females might differ significantly from males in the moral principles they used in arriving at moral decisions, we found that there was only a slight tendency in certain situations for females to appear more compassionate and caring than males in the consequences they recommended for wrongdoers. We concluded that the magnitude of the observed differences between females and males in the present study was too small to warrant broadscale conclusions about possible gender differences in the principles on which people ground their moral judgments. It appears that the moral principles and conditions to which people subscribe form complex patterns that differ from one individual to another, patterns that cannot adequately be interpreted in terms of gender differences.

The 20 interviews that followed the opinionnaire survey were used to clarify questions about cognitive style that remained unresolved by the survey. The analysis of opinionnaires showed the consequences people recommended in the six cases of wrongdoing. The survey had also revealed some of the considerations people weighed in arriving at their final decision, but the survey was not suited to delineating the styles of reasoning that people employed in arriving at their judgments. The tape-recorded interviews, however, did furnish the appropriate information. To elicit the desired data, the interviews were designed around a series of questions focusing on the taxonomy's five major categories.

From the analysis of the interviews, we prepared a written profile of overt moral-reasoning style (called a *response portrait*) to reflect the essence of a particular respondent's mode of recommending and defending consequences for misdeeds. The portrait centered on six dimensions of reasoning style labeled (1) overt reasoning process, (2) intuition versus logical argument, (3) fertility of options, (4) strength of ultimate conviction, (5) displayed emotionality, and (6) semantic disagreement. We suggested that the style a person displayed could affect the reaction that listeners might exhibit toward the consequence proposals that person was espousing.

APPLICATIONS OF THE TAXONOMY

Four of the ways the taxonomy can be used in solving practical problems are as an aid in values-clarification activities, in the evaluation of instruction, in the selection of judges, and in the diagnosis of clients' thought patterns during counseling and psychotherapy.

Encouraging Values Clarification

In the popular approach to moral education known as values clarification, learners are usually asked to offer their opinions about hypothetical or real-life cases of moral decision. Values-clarification programs can be distinguished from values-indoctrination programs in terms of their purpose. The intent of values indoctrination is to convince people to accept the values advocated by those in charge of the program. In contrast, the intent of values clarification is to equip people to determine their own values instead of automatically accepting values urged on them by others (Krathwohl, Bloom, & Masia, 1964; Raths, Harmin, & Simon, 1964; Thomas, 1988b).

Sometimes a case being studied during a values-clarification activity depicts a completed moral-decision confrontation. For instance, the case might involve a judge sentencing a bank robber to prison for 10 years. The learners' task is to tell whether they concur with the judge's decision and then to defend their position on the grounds of values they hold. On other occasions the values-clarification case will describe a moral conflict only up to the point at which a decision needs to be made. Learners are then asked to tell how they think the conflict should be resolved and why they consider their solution is a good one. For example, a college student is caught cheating on a final examination in a mathematics class. Learners are asked what should be done about the student and why such a consequence is more suitable than other options.

The taxonomy described in Part II of this volume can be used for categorizing learners' responses to the cases being studied. That is, each student's response can be dissected into the components defined by the taxonomy—underlying moral principles, conditions affecting the application of the principles in this particular case, the purpose to be served by the proposed consequences, likely causes of the misdeeds in the case, reasons that the recommended consequence is expected to achieve its purpose (causal process), feasibility considerations, and identification of agents who are deemed qualified to suggest and to impose the consequences.

When several students' responses to the same case are thus analyzed into their constituent elements, learners are able to recognize specific ways in which they agree and disagree with each other in their value judgments. As they discuss the likenesses and differences, they have an opportunity to explain in terms of the taxonomy categories why they subscribed to the values they have adopted. This act of rationalizing their beliefs not only helps them understand more clearly the process they have intuitively followed in assigning consequences, but it often motivates people to alter their beliefs as a result of hearing other people's reasons for their consequence proposals. In effect, the taxonomy furnishes a structure for the analysis of the values embedded in people's modes of reasoning about consequences.

Evaluating the Effect of Treatments

A typical method of evaluating the effect of instruction is commonly referred to as the *pretest-treatment-posttest* approach. The method involves (a) assessing the learners' knowledge, skills, or attitudes prior to the start of instruction, (b) providing the instruction, then (c) assessing the learners' knowledge, skills, or attitudes at the close of instruction. The taxonomy can serve such an evaluation device in the following manner.

First, the learners are presented a case of wrongdoing and asked to answer questions focusing on one or more of the components of the taxonomy. Such questions could include ones from the beginning of Chapter 10. The students' answers are collected and held until the close of the instructional program.

The program is then carried out. At its close, the learners are presented with another case of wrongdoing whose characteristics are similar to the initial case they had been asked to judge. Again they are asked the questions they faced during the pretest.

Finally, each learner's pretest and posttest answers are scored in terms of the taxonomy categories. In other words, the answers are analyzed to reveal which of the items under each category are included, either by direct statement or by implication. Then the pattern of the scored items from the person's pretest is compared with the pattern from his or her posttest to identify any changes in values that occurred between the beginning and the end of the instructional period. Changes observed in the answers of individual students can subsequently be summed to furnish a picture of change for the entire group of learners. The instructional program is usually credited as the likely cause of such changes, or at least part of the cause.

It is obviously unnecessary to use the entire taxonomy when evaluating the effects of a treatment or intervention. The instructor may be interested in only one or two aspects of the taxonomy, such as the purposes that students intend a consequence to achieve or the conditions students include when applying moral principles in cases of wrongdoing. On these occasions, only the purposes section or the conditions section of the taxonomy is used in evaluating the learner's answers.

Selecting Judges

A further way the taxonomy can be applied is in the selection of people to judge cases of wrongdoing and to recommend the sanctions or treatments that wrongdoers should experience. The aim of using the taxonomy during such a selection process would be to indicate how closely a potential judge's moral values and manner of moral reasoning match the values and line of logic advocated by the group for which the judge would serve.

Many types of groups engage in such a selection process. Such is the case when the voting public elects judges for the court system, law firms hire attorneys and paralegal personnel, officials in the judicial system appoint parole officers, trial lawyers select jury members, social-service agencies employ social workers, school boards hire administrators and teachers, police departments recruit new officers, political parties nominate candidates to run for public office, and more.

The method of applying the taxonomy for such a purpose can follow much the same procedure as the one used for interviewing respondents in the present study, as described in Chapter 10. For example, candidates for the position of judge would read or listen to a case of wrongdoing, then be asked which of several consequence options they would endorse—or perhaps they would prefer to suggest a different consequence. Candidates next would be asked questions designed to reveal their moral values and the pattern of reasoning they have followed in arriving at their decision. These probing queries would likely include one or more of the questions listed at the opening of Chapter 10. Candidates' answers could then be assessed for both their content (as defined by the items listed in Chapters 3 through 5) and their style (as defined by the six aspects of style described in Chapter 10). The results of the analysis would be used for estimating how closely each candidate's values and style corresponded to the preferences of the group conducting the assessment.

Facilitating Psychotherapeutic Diagnosis

With certain types of counseling and psychotherapy clients, the taxonomy can serve as a diagnostic tool. Such clients are ones who consider themselves victims of mistreatment, and they have in mind consequences they think should be faced by the person or group they consider responsible for their plight. Clients of this variety include married persons in the midst of separation or divorce, abused children, battered wives, individuals who have suffered such casualties as rape or auto accidents, victims of exploitation or fraud, workers who have lost their jobs, and the like.

The taxonomy can be included among the diagnostic devices a therapist employs to reveal clients' values and their perceptions of their alleged oppressors. One way to use the taxonomy for this purpose is to ask the person what he or she would like to see happen to the individual or group that has been the ostensible cause of the client's ill fate. This initial query can then be followed with questions selected from the list in Chapter 10 as a means of exposing specific aspects of the individual's reasoning process.

As a second option, the therapist may prefer not to confront the client initially with the client's own problem but, instead, may begin with a hypothetical case, one similar to the client's situation. The individual would be asked to propose a consequence for the wrongdoer in the illustrative case and to explain such things as the objectives to be gained by the consequence, why the consequence would achieve its purpose, and who should carry out the consequence.

Within each of the above approaches, the client's responses would be interpreted in terms of the taxonomy components described in Part II. Items under the separate sections of the taxonomy could also become the source of topics to be discussed with the client. For example, drawing on the list of purposes in Chapter 4, the counselor might suggest, "You said you'd like to see your ex-husband spend some time in jail for the way he's treated you. Is there anything else you would want jail to accomplish besides—as you expressed it— 'Keeping him from doing it again'? Would one of your purposes in locking him up be to make him suffer, to be paid back for what you've suffered?" Or, as another option, the therapist might draw once more from the list of purposes in the taxonomy and ask, "Would you want him somehow to compensate you for your pain and loss? If so, what sort of compensation would you expect, and why would you choose that kind?"

RESEARCH PROSPECTS

As a final step, we consider several research possibilities that can be generated from our investigation of what wrongdoers deserve.

Perhaps the most obvious activity for extending the present study is that of expanding and refining our initial version of the taxonomy by using other cases and populations of respondents than those we used. Additional cases that would appear useful for enriching the taxonomy categories are ones centering on sexual behavior, fraud, freedom of choice, gender roles, property rights, religious rights, the treatment of animals, misrepresentation in advertising and sales, fair versus unfair competition, misconduct in political office, and employer-employee relations.

A limitation of the opinionnaire survey used in the present study was that it failed to reveal the entire range of moral principles, conditions, and purposes that respondents considered when proposing consequences. Rather, the survey appeared to elicit only those few aspects of the cases that occurred to respondents at the moment. Furthermore, by asking participants only a general question about the reasons for their consequence choice ("Why is your choice a good one?"), the opinionnaire failed to extract respondents' opinions about every part of the taxonomy. The interviews conducted following the survey corrected this weakness, because specific queries were directed at each portion in turn. However, the interviews still did not plumb participants' modes of reasoning in sufficient depth.

In order to remedy this shortcoming, we propose that future research in this domain could profit from an added methodological feature. First, the collection of data would begin with the same interview procedure as that used in the present investigation. Then, after a respondent's opinions about each section of the taxonomy had been elicited by means of the eight guide questions, the interviewer would search more thoroughly through that respondent's thought processes by displaying a series of lists for the respondent to inspect. Each list would contain items from one segment of the taxonomy. The first list would consist of moral principles; the second, of conditions; the third, of purposes; and so on. The respondent's task would be to select from each list those items to which he or she subscribed when proposing a consequence for the case at hand.

For example, when asked the purpose that a proposed jail sentence would serve, an interviewee may have only said that it would prevent the offender from repeating the misdeed. However, when confronted with a list of other possible purposes, the respondent might intend the sanction to achieve additional aims as well—wreak revenge, cause the wrongdoer pain, deter others from committing the same offense, reform the wrongdoer, teach accountability, and protect society. In brief, adding such lists in the conduct of the interview can reveal further details of people's patterns of thought. However, the use of such lists is not without disadvantages. The task of judging the lists markedly extends the time required for the interview, thereby contributing to fatigue on the part of both interviewer and respondent.

As a final suggestion of research possibilities, we propose the following questions as ones that might profitably be answered through additional studies in this field.

Moral Principles: In various cases of wrongdoing, which principles are mutually supportive, which are in conflict, and why? As a respondent decides on a suitable consequence, which principles does the respondent value more than others? In other words, which principles are considered more important or more powerful than others, and why? How may principles vary from one case to another? How consistently does an individual give priority to a given principle from one case to another, and what are the circumstances that influence the degree of consistency?

Conditions Affecting the Application of Moral Principles: Which conditions take priority over others in the determination of consequences in various kinds of cases? How may the conditions people cite vary by the age of the respondents?

Purposes: What scheme for organizing purposes would be more profitable than the three-level hierarchy employed in the present study?

Causes: As guides to understanding people's moral-reasoning processes, are there more appropriate theories or interpretations of cause than the ones used in our study of just deserts? To what degree, and in what manner, do accounts of cause differ in relation to the age level of respondents? In other words, are there developmental changes in proposals about the causes of wrongdoing?

CONCLUSION

In this final chapter we have identified several practical applications of the taxonomy that was described in Part II. We have also suggested a number of issues that can usefully be pursued in future research projects. As those suggestions imply, we believe the taxonomy is still far from complete. In its present form, it represents only a step along the way toward understanding the moral reasoning behind people's suggestions of consequences for wrongdoing.

References

Bandura, A. (1969). *Principles of behavior modification.* New York: Holt, Rinehart, & Winston.

Bandura, A. (1977). *Social learning theory.* Englewood Cliffs, NJ: Prentice-Hall.

Cortès, J. B., & Gatti, F. M. (1972). *Delinquency and crime.* New York: Seminar Press.

Freud, S. (1973). *An outline of psychoanalysis.* London: Hogarth. (Original work published 1938)

Gert, B. (1970). *The moral rules—A new rational foundation for morality.* New York: Harper & Row.

Gilligan, C. (1982). *In a different voice.* Cambridge, MA: Harvard University Press.

Gilligan, C., Ward, J. V., & Taylor, J. M. (Eds.). (1988). *Mapping the moral domain.* Cambridge, MA: Harvard University Press.

Gleuck, S., & Gleuck, E. (1950). *Unraveling juvenile delinquency.* New York: Commonwealth Fund.

Gleuck, S., & Gleuck, E. (1956). *Physique and delinquency.* New York: Harper & Brothers.

Gleuck, S., & Gleuck, E. (1974). *Of delinquency and crime.* Springfield, IL: Thomas.

Hollin, C. R. (1990). *Cognitive-behavioral interventions with young offenders.* Oxford: Pergamon.

Holy Bible. (1611). King James authorized edition. Philadelphia: Winston, 1930.

Kohlberg, L. (1984). *The psychology of moral development.* San Francisco: Harper & Row.

Krathwohl, D. R., Bloom, B. S., & Masia, B. B. (1964). *Taxonomy of educational objectives—Handbook II: Affective domain.* New York: Mckay.

Kretschmer, R. (1921). *Physique and character* (W. J. H. Sprott, Translator.). New York: Cooper Square Publishers. (Reprinted, 1936)

Marx, K. (1959). A contribution to the critique of political economy. In L. S. Feuer (Ed.), *Karl Marx and Friedrich Engels: Basic writing on politics and philosophy.* Garden City, NY: Anchor/Doubleday.

Noddings, N. (1984). *Caring.* Berkeley: University of California Press.

Piaget, J. (1966). *The moral judgment of the child* (M. Gabain, Translator.). Glencoe, IL: Free Press. (Original work published 1932)

Raths, L. E., Harmin, M., & Simon, S. B. (1964). *Values and teaching.* Columbus, OH: Merrill.

Ray, D., & Tarrow, N. B. (1987). Human rights and education: An overview. In N. B. Tarrow (Ed.). *Human rights and education* (pp. 3-16). Oxford: Pergamon.

Ryan, M. (1991, September 1). Did the judge go too far? *Parade Magazine,* pp. 8-9.

Sheldon, W. H. (1940). *Varieties of physique.* New York: Harper & Brothers.

Sheldon, W. H. (1942). *Varieties of temperament.* New York: Harper & Brothers.

Sheldon, W. H. (1949). *Varieties of delinquent youth.* New York: Harper & Brothers.

Shoemaker, D. J. (1990). *Theories of delinquency* (2nd ed.). New York: Oxford University Press.

Skinner, B. F. (1969). *Contingencies of reinforcement: A theoretical analysis.* Englewood Cliffs, NJ: Prentice-Hall.

Skinner, B. F. (1974). *About behaviorism.* New York: Knopf.

Thomas, R. M. (Ed.). (1988a). *Oriental theories of human development.* New York: Peter Lang.

Thomas, R. M. (1988b). Values goals and affective goals in general education. In I. Westbury & A. C. Purves (Eds.), *Cultural literacy and the idea of general education* (NSSE Eighty-Seventh Yearbook, Part II, pp. 149-170). Chicago: National Society for the Study of Education.

Thomas, R. M. (1989). A proposed taxonomy of moral values. *Journal of Moral Education, 18* (1), 60-72.

Wilson, E. O. (1978). *On human nature.* Cambridge, MA: Harvard University Press.

Index

About the Authors

R. MURRAY THOMAS is a professor emeritus from the Graduate School of Education at the University of California, Santa Barbara. He is the author of more than 275 articles and books on educational psychology and comparative education.

ANN DIVER-STAMNES is an assistant professor in the Teacher Preparation Program at California's Humboldt State University. She has published in the areas of adolescent development, multicultural education, peer counseling, and education in urban areas.